Drywall

Drywall

Professional Techniques for Great Results

Revised and Updated

MYRON R. FERGUSON

The Taunton Press

The Taunton Press
Inspiration for hands-on living®

Printed in the United States of America

20 19 18 17 16 15 14 13 12

For Pros by Pros® is a trademark of The Taunton Press, Inc., registered in the U.S. Patent and Trademark Office.

The Taunton Press, Inc.

63 South Main Street

P.O. Box 5506

Newtown, CT 06470-5506

e-mail: tp@taunton.com

Cover designer: Cathy Cassidy

Interior designer and layout artist: Jeff Potter/Potter Publishing Studio

Illustrator: Scott Bricher

Library of Congress Cataloging-in-Publication Data

Ferguson, Myron R.

  Drywall : professional techniques for great results / Myron R. Ferguson.-- Rev. and updated.

      p. cm.

Includes index.

  ISBN-13: 978-1-56158-529-8

  ISBN-10: 1-56158-529-7

 1. Drywall construction. 2. Drywall. I. Title.

 TH2239 .F47 2002

 690'.12--dc21   2002000248

To Amber, Brandon, and Christopher: my pride and joy.

ACKNOWLEDGMENTS

Prior to writing the first edition of this book, most of what I learned throughout my years in the drywall trade was through trial and error along with some research into new products and tools. Since the initial publication, new tools and techniques have emerged, and a great deal of information has crossed my desk. Thanks to all the companies that asked my opinion about a new tool or material. It is great to see that so many people are always thinking of ways to improve the trade that I love so much.

I'd like to thank all the folks at The Taunton Press who've worked with me and believed in me enough to make the revised edition possible. Thanks to all the gypsum companies who sent me information and to the Gypsum Association for providing me with the material on the levels of drywall finishing. I am also grateful for all the people who let me use

their homes or equipment for the photo shoots. And I must thank my subcontractors Jeff, Ira, and Chris (you'll see them in photos throughout the book). Many times I left them with all the work while I got ready for a photo session, talked to my editor, or did one of the many other tasks that have to happen to make a book possible.

And finally, a huge thanks to my wife, Linda, who worked with me many late nights and weekends doing all the computer work, offering editorial suggestions, and keeping me on schedule. I also thank my three wonderful children, Amber, Brandon, and Christopher, for being very patient with me. I know there were many times when they would rather have heard about anything else but drywall. My older son, Brandon, has actually started referring to me as That Drywall Guy. I like it.

Contents

Introduction   2

1 Drywall Basics   4

Types and Uses of Drywall   5

Planning the Job   13

2 Tools and Materials   22

Hanging Tools   23

Taping Tools and Materials   38

Sanding Tools and Materials   46

3 Hanging Drywall   48

Backing Materials   49

Measuring and Cutting Drywall   51

General Guidelines for Hanging Drywall   59

Fastening Drywall   59

Hanging Ceilings   63

Hanging Walls   67

Trim Accessories   74

4 Taping   78

Taping Basics   78

Taping Fastener Heads   83

Taping Seams   84

Taping Inside Corners   91

Taping Outside Corners   96

Skim Coating   99

Mechanical Taping   101

Taping Problems   104

5 Sanding   107

Getting Ready to Sand   108

The Sanding Process   109

Wet Sanding   115

6 Special Installations 117

Off-Angle Corners	**118**
Curved Walls	**123**
Archways	**124**
Butted Seams	**129**
Flat Taping	**132**
Applying L-Bead	**133**
Multilayer Applications	**134**
Installing Cement Board	**137**
Control Joints	**140**

7 Repairs 142

Popped Nails and Screws	**142**
Repairing Holes in Drywall	**144**
Remodeling Repairs	**149**
Stress Cracks	**154**
Water Damage	**155**

8 Decorating Drywall 158

Painting	**158**
Texturing	**162**
Wall Coverings	**170**

Appendix	171
Resources	174
Index	176

Introduction

Drywall, wallboard, Sheetrock®, gypsum board. . . call it what you will, this material is on more walls and ceilings than any other material in new construction. Drywall covers approximately 80% of the visible interior of a home, and it holds more than a 90% market share of interior finish materials. Properly installed and finished, drywall can add real beauty to a home or business. Improperly attached or finished, it can be a major eyesore. In this book, I'll teach you how to do it right, with techniques and materials used by the pros.

My first drywalling job was on my own house quite a few years ago. I'd heard a lot of negative things about the chore of installing drywall, but to my surprise I found that I liked the work. Hanging the panels provided me with the physical work that I enjoy, while taping and finishing drywall proved to be an interesting test of my patience and skill. When I started out in the business in

1980, I had a bare minimum of tools and a pretty limited knowledge of the drywall trade. But over the years, I've experimented with different kinds of drywall, joint tape, and joint compounds; added numerous tools to my drywalling arsenal; and studied the work of several professional hangers and tapers.

I'm still learning. Each year manufacturers bring out new materials, such as the variety of corner beads and tapes now on the market. These products not only improve productivity, they also enhance the finished look of the project. Tapers and hangers are always developing and honing installation techniques, and a whole rash of new application tools makes the work go more quickly and smoothly. No text on drywalling would be complete without them, so we decided to update the book with this new information. My experiences, including countless hours spent hanging and taping drywall, have enabled me to develop techniques that virtually guarantee success when drywalling.

If you've ever watched a professional hanger or taper in action, the work probably looked deceptively simple—panels are attached and joints taped in a graceful rhythm. But don't be deceived; working with drywall is not without its frustrations. Getting the perfect finish on the final coat of joint compound can be maddening, and finding a highly conspicuous ridge running the length of the ceiling after you've painted can all but reduce you to tears. Drywalling requires care and attention to detail at every step of the way. It requires knowing when to use one type of drywall rather than another, screws rather than nails, mesh rather than paper tape, and drying-type compound rather than setting-type compound.

Drywalling is a very linear process, and I've organized the book in roughly the order I handle a typical job—from

planning the layout to hanging, taping, and sanding drywall to finishing the walls and ceilings (with paint, textures, or wall coverings). I've also included a chapter on special installations (such as curved walls and double-layer applications) and another on drywall repairs. It's a complete course in drywalling.

CHAPTER 1

Drywall Basics

DURING THE 1940s and 1950s, prefabricated drywall panels gradually replaced plaster as the material of choice for finishing interior walls and ceilings. The earliest drywall panels were used to replace the lath backing in plasterwork; they were narrow (16 in. wide) and only ⅜ in. thick. Today, drywall comes in a wide variety of lengths, thicknesses, and special-use materials. The low cost and the large, easy-to-attach panels make drywall the preferred choice over conventional plaster.

A sheet of drywall consists of a hardened gypsum core sandwiched between two layers of paper—a strong, smooth-finished paper on one side (the face) and a rougher, "natural" paper on the back (see the drawing on the facing page). The face paper is folded around the long edges, which are tapered slightly to accommodate joint tape and compound after the panel is installed. The ends of the panel are cut square and finished smooth, leaving the gypsum core exposed.

Plaster-and-lath construction adds a lot of moisture to a building, and plastered surfaces must be left to dry for up to two weeks (depending on humidity, temperature, and airflow) before being decorated. By comparison, drywall has a low moisture content and the joint compounds used to finish the panels cover only a portion of the exterior, rather than the entire surface, so they dry in 24 hours or less—hence the name "drywall." Drywall is known by many other names, as well, such as Sheetrock (a brand name), gypsum board, plasterboard, wallboard, and gypsum drywall.

Drywall panels stacked on a truck wait to be unloaded.

Drywall provides excellent sound control, structural integrity, and fire resistance. It is easy to decorate and serves as a good base for paint, wallpaper, paneling, textured finishes, decorative fabric, and vinyl wall coverings. The generic term *drywall* refers to a number of different types of panels, each with characteristics that make it suitable for specific residential and commercial applications.

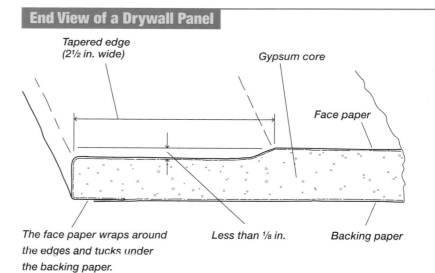

End View of a Drywall Panel

Tapered edge (2½ in. wide)

Gypsum core

Face paper

Less than ⅛ in.

Backing paper

The face paper wraps around the edges and tucks under the backing paper.

Types and Uses of Drywall

When most people think of drywall, they probably picture the standard 4×8 panel that has been in use since drywall first became popular. But this is by no means the only size or type of drywall available today. Panels come in lengths of up to 16 ft. and in 48-in. and 54-in. widths. A wide variety of special-use drywall is also available, including moisture-resistant, fire-resistant, and abuse-resistant panels; ¼-in. flexible panels; ½-in. high-strength ceiling panels; and foil-backed panels. In this section, I'll guide you through the various types and their uses, the thicknesses and lengths available, and the framing specifications for each one. With this information, you'll be able to make the right decision about which type of drywall to order when it comes time to plan a job.

Regular drywall

Regular drywall panels are 48 in. wide and come in a variety of lengths, ranging from 8 ft. to 16 ft. (see the chart on p. 6). Panels are available in four thicknesses— ⅝ in., ½ in., ⅜ in., and ¼ in.—and each one has specific applications and framing requirements.

Drywall panels are available in a number of sizes and thicknesses. The larger panel shown here is 54 in. wide.

FIVE-EIGHTH-INCH REGULAR DRY-WALL is the thickest regular drywall available and provides the best single-layer application over wood and metal framing on walls and ceilings. These panels have greater fire resistance and better sound control than the other thicknesses, and because the panels are

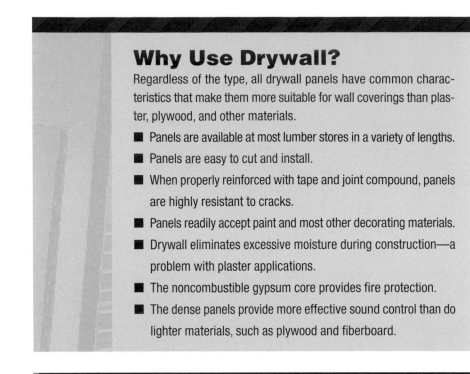

Why Use Drywall?

Regardless of the type, all drywall panels have common characteristics that make them more suitable for wall coverings than plaster, plywood, and other materials.

- Panels are available at most lumber stores in a variety of lengths.
- Panels are easy to cut and install.
- When properly reinforced with tape and joint compound, panels are highly resistant to cracks.
- Panels readily accept paint and most other decorating materials.
- Drywall eliminates excessive moisture during construction—a problem with plaster applications.
- The noncombustible gypsum core provides fire protection.
- The dense panels provide more effective sound control than do lighter materials, such as plywood and fiberboard.

Regular Drywall

Thickness	Common Uses	Available Lengths	Maximum Framing Spacing
⅝ in.	Walls and ceilings	8 ft., 9 ft., 10 ft., 12 ft., 14 ft.	24 in. o.c.; 16 in. o.c., if textured or hung parallel to ceiling joists
½ in.	Walls and ceilings (most common type of drywall used)	8 ft., 9 ft., 10 ft., 12 ft., 14 ft., 16 ft.	24 in. o.c.; 16 in. o.c., if textured or hung parallel to ceiling joists
⅜ in.	Remodeling, mainly on walls	8 ft., 10 ft., 12 ft.	16 in. o.c.
¼ in.	Remodeling over solid surfaces or curved surfaces with long radii	8 ft., 10 ft.	16 in. o.c. as double layer or as single layer over solid surfaces

stiffer they are more resistant to sagging. This drywall can be used on walls and ceilings with framing members (wall studs and ceiling joists) spaced up to 24 in. on center (o.c.). If you install (or "hang") the panels parallel to the ceiling joists, the joists should be no farther apart than 16 in. o.c. to prevent sagging. If you hang ⅝-in. panels perpendicular to the ceiling joists, a water-based textured coating can be applied only if the ceiling

joists are 16 in. o.c. or closer (again, to avoid sagging).

HALF-INCH REGULAR DRYWALL is the most commonly used drywall in both new construction and remodeling. It is usually used as a single layer over wood or metal framing; however, it can be installed in two layers (with staggered seams) to increase fire resistance and sound control. The framing requirements for ½-in. drywall are the same as for ⅝-in. panels. If the framing is farther apart than the recommended spacing, wood or metal furring strips can be attached across the framing to create the specified o.c. spacing.

THREE-EIGHTH-INCH REGULAR DRYWALL was initially used to replace wood lath as a backing for plaster. When drywall first became popular, ⅜-in. panels were widely used on walls and ceilings in new construction, but it was eventually replaced by the more durable ½-in. drywall. Today, ⅜-in. drywall is used mainly to cover existing surfaces in repair and remodeling work or to provide a backing for paneling. It is also used in double-layer applications. The maximum distance between framing members on walls and ceilings is 16 in. o.c. For installation on studs and joists that are more than 16 in. o.c. apart, install furring strips. Use a double layer of ⅜-in. drywall with adhesive applied between the two layers (see p. 134).

QUARTER-INCH REGULAR DRYWALL is a lightweight panel that is used to cover old walls and ceiling surfaces in remodeling jobs or to provide sound control in double-layer or multilayer applications. When hanging ¼-in. drywall over old plaster or drywall, use adhesive in combination with screws between the old surface and the new drywall to

Moisture-resistant drywall has a distinctive green face paper and a darker, moisture-resistant backing paper.

strengthen the panels and reduce sagging. These thin panels are too weak to install in a single layer over bare studs or joists without a backing.

Regular ¼-in. drywall is easily bent and can be used to form curved surfaces with long radii (5 ft. or more) if applied dry or shorter radii (3 ft. or more) if applied wet. A better choice for curved surfaces, however, is ¼-in. flexible drywall, which is discussed later in this chapter (see p. 10). Maximum o.c. framing for ¼-in. regular drywall (either as a double layer or as a single layer over an existing solid surface) is 16 in.

Moisture-resistant drywall

This drywall, which has a light-green or blue face paper to distinguish it from other types of drywall (hence the names greenboard and blueboard), is designed to minimize moisture problems. The panels are moisture-resistant all the way through and are made to withstand high humidity and low levels of moisture.

Moisture-resistant drywall is mainly used to cover bathrooms, the bottom 4 ft. of a laundry or utility room, or the wall behind a kitchen sink. It is an excellent base for ceramic, plastic, and metal tile applied with an adhesive, as well as for other nonabsorbent finishes, such as paint, wallpaper, and plastic tub surrounds.

Moisture-resistant drywall should not be used in a wet or high-moisture area, such as a shower enclosure or the wall just above a tub, unless it will be covered with ceramic tile or a tub

Moisture-Resistant Drywall

Thickness	Common Uses	Available Lengths	Maximum Framing Spacing
½ in.	Bathrooms; damp areas	8 ft., 10 ft., 12 ft. (up to 16 ft. as special order)	16 in. o.c. on walls; 12 in. o.c. on ceilings
⅝ in.	Bathroom ceilings; fire walls in damp or high-humidity areas	8 ft., 10 ft., 12 ft. (up to 16 ft. as special order)	16 in. o.c. on walls; 16 in. o.c. on ceilings

surround. In addition, moisture-resistant drywall should not be installed over a vapor retarder—including walls that act as vapor retarders—if it will later be finished with another vapor retarder material, such as ceramic tile, vinyl tub surround, vinyl wallpaper, or oil-based paint. The objective here is to avoid creating a double vapor retarder, which could eventually deteriorate the drywall if moisture were to become trapped by a water-resistant finish. Rather, moisture-resistant drywall should be attached directly to the framing. In areas that are not covered with tile or other wall coverings, moisture-resistant drywall can be taped and painted just like other types of drywall.

Moisture-resistant drywall, which is available in ½-in. regular or ⅝-in. fire-resistant panels, is used mainly as a wall covering over 16-in. o.c. framing. If you plan to install it on a ceiling, use ⅝-in. panels over 16-in. centers and ½-in. panels over 12-in. (or less) centers. (If the ceiling is insulated, make sure that

unfaced insulation was used to avoid creating a double vapor barrier.)

Fire-resistant drywall

As a dense, noncombustible, mineral-based material, drywall in all its forms is a better fire barrier and a more efficient sound absorber than lighter materials, such as plywood. Even better, fire-resistant drywall has a gypsum core with special additives and glass fibers that are particularly effective in containing fire. This drywall is a little harder to cut than regular drywall, because the gypsum core is tougher.

On the surface, these panels look the same as regular drywall, except for a stamp indicating that they are fire resistant. The term *fire resistance* means the ability of a constructed assembly (a wall or a ceiling covered with drywall) to contain a fire. The fire-resistance rating for each thickness of drywall is measured in intervals of time: 45 minutes for ½-in. fire-resistant drywall, 60 minutes for ⅝-in. panels, and 120 minutes for ¾-in. ones. The panels can be layered to increase the fire rating.

HALF-INCH FIRE-RESISTANT DRY-WALL. Many building codes specify fire-resistant drywall for attached garages, furnace or utility rooms, and ceilings and walls separating dwelling units in apartment and condominium complexes. The two most commonly used fire-resistant panels are ½ in. and ⅝ in. Half-in. panels are convenient when you need to cover only part of a wall or ceiling with fire-resistant drywall and finish the rest with regular ½-in. panels (the most common standard thickness). For example, a garage ceiling might be finished with two types of drywall. Typically, only the first 5 ft. of the ceiling adjacent to a house wall needs to be fire resistant. Using matching thicknesses allows you to make

■ WORK SAFE
■ WORK
■ THINKING AHEAD

When installing fire-resistant drywall on garage ceilings, use ⅝-in. panels. The joists are usually spaced 24 in. o.c., and ⅝-in. drywall isn't as likely to sag as ½-in. drywall is. On walls, the thicker panels resist dents better than the thinner materials do.

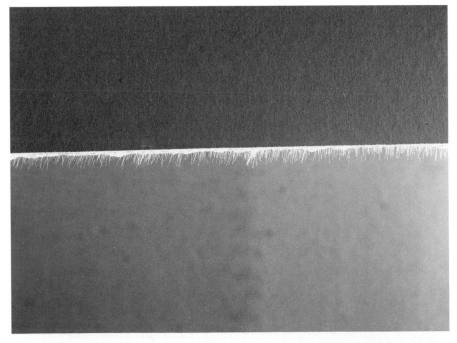

Fire-resistant drywall panels have gypsum cores with glass fibers that help contain fire.

a smooth transition at the joint. If you use different thicknesses (say, ⅝-in. fire resistant and ½-in. regular), you'll create a seam that's difficult to hide during the taping process.

FIVE-EIGHTH-INCH FIRE-RESISTANT DRYWALL. For fire resistance, ⅝-in. panels are the most commonly used size. They have the one-hour fire rating that many building codes require. Since most garage-ceiling joists are 24 in. o.c., ⅝-in. panels work best because they are approved for 24-in. spacing. Although manufacturers approve ½-in. panels for joists 24 in. o.c., they are more likely to sag, especially in a garage that is exposed to extremes in temperature and humidity. Because of the extra thickness and stronger core, ⅝-in. fire-resistant drywall stands up better to denting and other types of abuse than ½-in. drywall does. Since garages often suffer a lot of abuse from car doors, bikes, and tools, I like to cover the entire surface with ⅝-in. drywall.

Fire-Resistant Drywall

Thickness	Common Uses	Fire Rating	Available Lengths	Maximum Framing Spacing
½ in.	In areas where butted against regular ½ in.	45 min.	8 ft., 10 ft., 12 ft.	24 in. o.c.
⅝ in.	Garages; over 24-in. o.c. ceilings (most commonly used thickness)	60 min.	8 ft., 10 ft., 12 ft. (14 ft. as special order)	24 in. o.c.
¾ in.	Where high fire rating is required	120 min.	8 ft., 9 ft., 10 ft., 12 ft.	24 in. o.c.

THREE-QUARTER-INCH FIRE-RESISTANT DRYWALL. This type of drywall has a two-hour fire rating or a four-hour rating when the layers are doubled. It is used where a high fire rating is a must, such as to separate apartments or to divide offices from a garage or factory. The extra thickness and fire rating mean fewer layers, cutting down on the cost of materials and labor.

Abuse-resistant drywall is tougher than regular drywall and can hold up to heavy impacts.

Abuse-Resistant Drywall

Thickness	Common Uses	Available Lengths	Maximum Framing Spacing
½ in.	As an upgrade to regular drywall in high-traffic areas	8 ft., 10 ft., 12 ft.	24 in. o.c.
⅝ in.	As a fire wall in commercial and apartment buildings in high-traffic areas	8 ft., 10 ft., 12 ft.	24 in. o.c.

Abuse-resistant drywall

Abuse-resistant drywall is tougher than other types of drywall. It has a high-strength reinforced gypsum core sandwiched between smooth but thick abrasion-resistant paper on the face and heavy liner paper on the back. These products are called a variety of different names, including abuse-resistant, impact-resistant, and high-impact-resistant drywall. There are some advertisements that claim the panels are as tough as concrete. That's overdoing it, but they are tougher than both regular and fire-resistant panels. Despite their toughness, abuse-resistant panels can be finished like other types of drywall.

A garage wall is an ideal place for abuse-resistant drywall.

Abuse-resistant drywall holds up well in areas where regular drywall may be easily damaged, such as in mudrooms, workshops, garages, and other high-traffic areas. It is also more resistant to cracking and warping. This extra strength means long-term savings on repairs and replacement costs. Abuse-resistant drywall is available in ½-in. panels and ⅝-in. fire-resistant panels. The ⅝-in. fire-resistant panels are ideal in garages, utility rooms, and commercial work areas, where a high fire rating is necessary.

Quarter-inch flexible drywall

This drywall is designed for use on curved walls, archways, and stairways. It works well on both concave and convex surfaces. Flexible drywall has a heavier face paper and a stronger liner paper than regular ¼-in. drywall does, and it is easier to bend and more resistant to cracking caused by structural changes. It is usually

Flexible drywall panels are designed for use on archways and curved walls.

applied in double layers, with staggered seams where possible.

Not all curved surfaces have the same radius—some are tighter than others. For curved surfaces with a short radius (32 in. or less), it may be necessary to wet the drywall before trying to attach it. Use a sponge or roller to wet the surface to be compressed; this helps the drywall mold around the curve without breaking. (For more on this procedure, see chapter 6.)

Half-inch high-strength ceiling panels

This drywall has a reinforced gypsum core that increases resistance to sagging, a common problem when using regular ½-in. drywall on widely spaced framing or when applying water-based textured coatings over drywall. High-strength drywall is rigid enough to hang over 24-in. o.c. joists (rather than 16-in. o.c. joists, as I recommend for regular ½-in. drywall) and can be textured without fear of sagging. Half-in. high-strength drywall is available in lengths of 8 ft. and 12 ft. (lengths of up to 16 ft. can be specially ordered).

Foil-backed drywall

This drywall has aluminum foil laminated to the back of the panel. The foil creates an effective vapor barrier and adds to the insulating value of the drywall. It is used mainly in cold climates to help prevent interior moisture from entering wall and ceiling cavities.

Foil-backed drywall can be used over wood and metal framing, over furred masonry, or as the base layer for multilayer applications. It should not be used as a base for tile or highly moisture-resistant wall coverings, such as vinyl wallpaper, since the core could absorb and trap moisture and eventually damage the drywall. Foil-backed drywall is also not recommended for use in hot, humid climates. Panels are available in ⅜-in.,

Minimum Bending Radii of ¼-inch Flexible Drywall (Attached Lengthwise)

Type of Curve	Wet or Dry	Minimum Radius	Maximum Stud Spacing
Inside curve (concave)	Dry	32 in.	9 in. o.c.
Inside curve (concave)	Wet	20 in.	9 in. o.c.
Outside curve (convex)	Dry	32 in.	9 in. o.c.
Outside curve (convex)	Wet	15 in.	6 in. o.c.

½-in., and ⅝-in. thicknesses and in the same lengths as those for regular drywall.

54-inch-wide drywall

One of the main goals of hanging drywall is to have as few seams as possible. That's fine when hanging 4-ft.-wide sheets on walls with 8-ft. (or lower) ceilings, since the panels can be hung horizontally with just one seam (see p. 14 for an explanation of why I prefer to hang drywall horizontally rather than vertically). But more and more homes are being constructed with 9-ft.-high ceilings, which means that 4-ft.-wide drywall creates two horizontal seams on each wall.

The way to avoid the extra seam is to use 54-in.-wide drywall panels, which were introduced in the early 1990s for use on 9-ft.-high ceilings. Fifty-four-in. drywall comes in regular ½-in. and ⅝-in. fire-resistant panels. Sheets are readily available in 12-ft. lengths, but lengths from 8 ft. to 16 ft. can be ordered. Fifty-four-in. drywall has the same framing specifications as those for regular 4-ft.-wide panels.

Cement board

Designed for areas exposed to water or high levels of moisture, cement board is an excellent base for tiled walls and floors and for the lower portions of a bathtub or shower enclosure. Unlike the materials discussed up to this point, cement board

▪ **WORK SAFE**
▪ **WORK SMART**
▪ **THINKING AHEAD**

Need to cover a 9-ft.-high wall? Use 54-in.-wide drywall and install it perpendicular to the studs. This method cuts down on the number of seams. You may need to special-order the drywall, but it is worth the extra trouble.

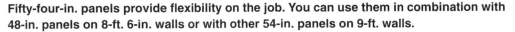

Fifty-four-in. panels provide flexibility on the job. You can use them in combination with 48-in. panels on 8-ft. 6-in. walls or with other 54-in. panels on 9-ft. walls.

is not a gypsum product; it has a cement core covered with fiberglass mesh. One side is rough, the other is smooth (see the photo below). The rough side, designed for mortar application of tile, increases bonding and decreases tile slippage. The smooth side is designed for mastic application of tile.

Cement board is commonly available in ½-in. and ⅝-in. panels. Standard widths are 32 in., 36 in., and 48 in.; the standard length is 5 ft., although 8-ft. panels are also available. The maximum stud spacing for cement board is 16 in. o.c. Panels should be attached with special screws or galvanized roofing nails, not with drywall screws or nails. (For more on installing cement board, see p. 137.) Cement board is quite fragile, so it should be stored flat to prevent warping and handled as carefully as possible.

Gypsum-core tile backer

This type of drywall consists of a silicone-treated core covered with a glass mat on both sides for added strength. The face has an acrylic coating, which serves as a vapor barrier. These panels, available in ½-in. and ⅝-in. thicknesses, are strong; lightweight; and easy to cut, snap, and fasten. Gypsum-core tile backer is recommended for residential and light commercial use as an underlayment for ceramic tile. It is used in many of the same areas as cement board. Although not as durable as cement board, gypsum-core tile backer is easier to work with and is available in larger sizes (4×8 and 5×8). Framing specifications are the same as those for cement board.

Cement board, which has one smooth side and one rough side, is used primarily as an underlayment for tile in areas exposed to water.

Planning the Job

Planning a drywall job involves more than just selecting the right type of drywall. You'll also need to estimate materials, make sure the materials (especially the longer-length panels) are available when needed, plan access for the drywall, and make sure you have enough help on the job site to maneuver the cumbersome panels. But before you start figuring out a material list for the job, there are some basic layout principles that you should keep in mind.

General layout guidelines

No two drywall projects are exactly alike, and each presents a unique set of challenges. But I've found that keeping the following items in mind helps just about any job go smoothly.

ALWAYS THINK OF WAYS TO ELIMINATE UNNECESSARY JOINTS when planning the layout of a room. Use the longest panels possible; remember that most types of drywall are available in lengths of up to 14 ft. or 16 ft. You may be tempted to use all 8-ft. lengths because they are lighter and easier to handle (and often cheaper), but don't. Using all 8-ft. panels creates too many seams that are difficult to hide. Keep in mind that fewer seams means less taping.

CEILING PANELS CAN BE ATTACHED either perpendicular to the ceiling joists (my preference) or parallel to the joists. Make sure that the type of drywall you intend to use is approved for the stud or joist spacing; drywall is stronger in the long direction (see the sidebar on p. 66). In addition, the framing spacing may affect the direction in which the drywall is hung.

Gypsum-core tile backer, which is used as an underlayment for tile, has a silicone-treated core sandwiched between layers of glass mat. The face of the panel has an acrylic coating.

ALWAYS TRY TO AVOID BUTTED SEAMS. A butted seam is a joint created when two untapered panel ends are joined together on the same framing member. If you have to use butted seams, stagger them as far as possible from the center of the wall. For example, if a wall is 8 ft. high by 20 ft. long, it is not a good idea to use four 10-ft. panels (see the drawing on p. 14). You'll end up with more than two butted seams on one wall or with seams on the same stud in the center of the wall. Instead, order two 16-ft. panels and one 8-ft. panel, and arrange them as shown in the drawing on p. 14. This way, there are only two butted seams on the wall and they're away from the center, where they are easier to hide when taping and finishing.

Placement of Butted Seams

Butted seams (at the panel ends) are on different studs and as far as possible from the center of the wall.

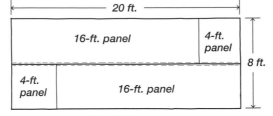

The right way

Butted seams are staggered but there are too many, and one is in the center of the wall.

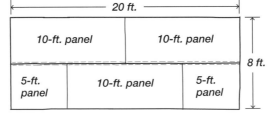

Too many butted seams

Butted seams are on the same stud and in the center of the wall.

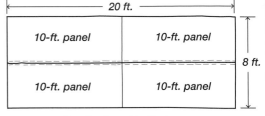

Poorly placed butted seams

Horizontal vs. Vertical Layout

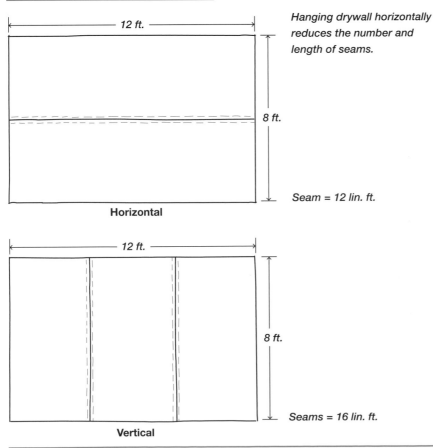

Horizontal

Vertical

Hanging drywall horizontally reduces the number and length of seams.

Seam = 12 lin. ft.

Seams = 16 lin. ft.

ON WALLS THAT ARE 4 FT. WIDE or less, hang the panels parallel to the studs (standing on end) to avoid a seam.

ON WALLS THAT ARE MORE THAN 4 FT. WIDE and no higher than 8 ft., hang the drywall horizontally (perpendicular to the studs). This technique reduces the linear footage of joints and also places the horizontal joints at a good height for taping (see the drawing at left).

FOR WALLS THAT ARE MORE THAN 8 FT. HIGH, consider using 54-in.-wide drywall panels, which can greatly reduce the linear footage of seams. Fifty-four-in.-wide drywall is available in lengths of up to only 12 ft. That could be a problem in larger rooms or areas where the walls are over 9 ft. high. In those cases, it may be better to install the drywall parallel to the studs. The goal is to use whichever method produces the fewest seams (measured in linear feet) to tape.

Sample Material List

Date: _____

Job name: _____

Location: ☐ downstairs   ☐ upstairs   ☐ garage   ☐ other _____

Regular Drywall ½ in.	
length	total
8 ft.	
10 ft.	
12 ft.	
14 ft.	
16 ft.	

Fire-Resistant Drywall ☐ ⅝ in. ☐ ½ in.	
length	total
8 ft.	
10 ft.	
12 ft.	
14 ft.	

Corner Bead	
length	total
8 ft.	
10 ft.	

Moisture-Resistant Drywall ½ in.	
length	total
8 ft.	
10 ft.	
12 ft.	
14 ft.	

Other	**Thickness**
length	total
8 ft.	
10 ft.	
12 ft.	
14 ft.	

Special instructions: _____

_____

_____

_____

_____

When filling out a material list, there are many ways to keep a tally of the number of sheets of drywall you'll need. I like to use the "dot tally" method—it takes up little space and doesn't require erasing if you make mistakes. Here's the key to the dot-tally system:

•	= 1	⌐∙	= 6
• •	= 2	⊔	= 7
∙ ∙	= 3	▢	= 8
∙∙ ∙∙	= 4	◺	= 9
⌊∙ ∙∙	= 5	⊠	= 10

If you put a dot in the wrong place, simply circle it. For example,

indicates 9 instead of 10.

Estimating materials

On most drywalling jobs, I figure out a rough material list from the blueprints and job specifications. I use this information to estimate the cost of the job. Once the building is framed, I obtain my exact material list by measuring the actual walls and ceilings.

Measuring the walls and ceilings makes it easier to visualize how to hang the drywall, decide which lengths and types to use, and figure out where to hang them. As I measure each room, I write down exactly what I'll need on a material list, using a separate list for each story of the building (see the sample material list on p. 15). The material list makes it easy to calculate the square footage of drywall, which helps me estimate the cost for the entire job (I usually estimate a job by the square foot). From the square footage, I can calculate the approximate amount of screws, nails, joint tape, joint compound, and paint needed to complete the job (see the sidebar on p. 45).

When working up the material list, I usually round lengths of walls and heights of ceilings to the next highest 2-ft.-length panel. For example, if a wall is 12 ft. 9 in. long, I order a 14-ft. panel (see the drawing below). In this example, the lower 4 ft. of the wall is broken up by a doorway, so I would order a 10-ft. panel to complete each side of the doorway with a minimum amount of waste. Always keep in mind that the idea is to use panels that span the entire length of the wall or ceiling whenever possible.

The drawing on the facing page shows how I estimate drywall for an entire room. In this particular example, I can use one length (16 ft.) for the wall with the window, since the window doesn't go all the way to the ceiling or the floor and the wall is less than 16 ft. long. On the ceiling, I can use either three 16-ft. panels or four 12-ft. panels. In this example, I'd choose the four 12-ft. panels, because it's preferable to attach the panels perpendicular to the ceiling joists (see p. 66) and the shorter lengths are easier to handle.

Sample Wall Layout

The most efficient way to drywall on this wall is to use one 14-ft. panel (top) and one 10-ft. panel (bottom). Hanging the drywall horizontally requires the fewest seams and produces the best-looking job.

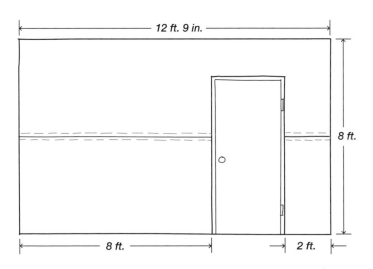

Sample Room Estimate

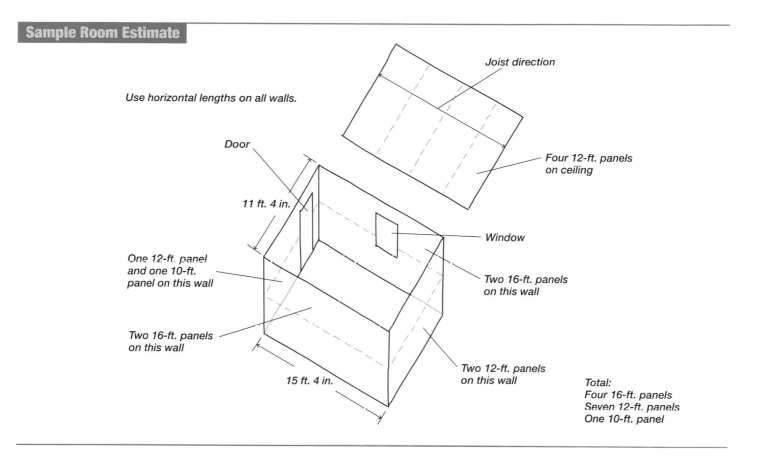

Use horizontal lengths on all walls.

Joist direction

Four 12-ft. panels on ceiling

Door

11 ft. 4 in.

Window

One 12-ft. panel and one 10-ft. panel on this wall

Two 16-ft. panels on this wall

Two 16-ft. panels on this wall

Two 12-ft. panels on this wall

15 ft. 4 in.

Total:
Four 16-ft. panels
Seven 12-ft. panels
One 10-ft. panel

ESTIMATING MATERIALS FOR AN ENTIRE HOUSE. When I'm working up a material list for a job, I usually don't need to figure out a separate list for each room—I know to use the maximum length possible for each wall. If a room is 12 ft. by 16 ft., I mainly use 12-ft. or 16-ft.-long panels, unless a doorway allows me to use a shorter length.

As I walk through a house, I note any rooms that will require special treatment. In the example shown in the plans on p. 21, the upstairs master bedroom has a cathedral ceiling, so I need to allow extra drywall for the ceiling and the gable ends. It's not a good idea to plan a butted seam directly under the ridge beam on the ends of a cathedral ceiling—there could be structural weight and some movement or settling, which would eventually cause the seam to crack—so I figure on spanning the end wall with 16-ft. panels.

In addition, cement board or tile backer will need to be used in the shower area of the master bathroom. I would also plan for the rest of the bathroom walls to be covered with ½-in. moisture-resistant drywall and the ceiling to be covered with ⅝-in. moisture-resistant panels.

The garage ceiling joists are 24 in. o.c., so I would estimate the entire ceiling using ⅝-in. fire-resistant drywall. All the garage walls adjacent to the house will need ⅝-in. fire-resistant drywall, too; for the rest of the garage I'd use regular ½-in. drywall. The garage walls are 10 ft. high, so I'd stand 10-ft. panels on end to avoid butted seams and to keep the linear footage of seams to a minimum (see p. 14).

After tallying the number and types of drywall panels needed, the next step is to calculate the total square footage of drywall required. Multiply the number of panels needed for each length by the square footage in one panel, and then add all the totals together. For example, the total square footage of drywall needed for the house shown in the plans is displayed in the chart below.

ROUGH-ESTIMATING A HOUSE. A quicker but less accurate way to estimate the amount of drywall needed for a house is to multiply the square footage of the living-area floor space for each story by 3.5. (I use this method to give a rough estimate over the phone, for example.) In the house in our example, multiplying the square footage of the upstairs and downstairs living areas (1,984 sq. ft.) by 3.5 gives a rough drywall total of 6,944 sq. ft. We also need to add the total for the garage. Multiply the total length of the garage walls by the height (112 ft. × 10 ft. = 1,120 sq. ft.), and then add the ceiling (approximately 700 sq. ft.): 1,120 + 700 = 1,820 sq. ft.

Using the rough estimating method, the total square footage of drywall needed for this house works out to be 8,764 sq. ft. (6,944 + 1,820). This figure is reasonably close to the actual square footage needed (9,128 sq. ft.) and a lot quicker to calculate.

For a house with 9-ft.-high ceilings, use 3.82 as the multiplier. Many houses have 8-ft.-high ceilings upstairs and 9-ft.-high ceilings downstairs. In those cases, calculate each floor separately and then add the totals together to obtain the rough estimate.

Planning access for materials

When calculating a material list for any building, you need to consider which lengths you can get into the building and the best way to get them inside (ideally, the contractor should start thinking about this before the framing begins). For a normal single-story building, access is generally not a concern. For anything over one story, you may need to make some special arrangements. Here are some ways to help plan for the best access:

1. Measure and inspect the job site before the rough framing is complete.
2. If necessary, ask the builder to leave out a window, a door, or even a section of plywood on an exterior wall to allow access for long panels.
3. Make note of overhead wires that could get in the way of a boom-truck delivery.
4. Look for freshly covered ditches or septic tanks, which may not support a heavy truck.
5. Note good areas to stack the drywall once it is delivered.

If you need to make special arrangements for access, watch the timing. Sometimes these arrangements are only available for a short period, so if you must special-order materials, do it early. Also, check out the job site to make sure there are appropriate areas to place all the drywall panels. The panels can be laid flat on the floor or on edge against a wall (make sure they are almost straight, so that they don't develop a bow, but not so straight that they will topple).

If you have a choice, stack them on the floor. The panels will stay flat and

Calculating Total Square Footage

Length	# Panels Needed		Square Footage of Each Panel		Total Square Footage
8 ft.	40	×	32	=	1,280
10 ft.	90	×	40	=	3,600
12 ft.	39	×	48	=	1,872
14 ft.	31	×	56	=	1,736
16 ft.	10	×	64	=	640
					9,128 sq. ft.

If there is a large enough opening in an exterior wall, a drywall boom truck can make quick work of a second- or third-story delivery.

■ **WORK SAFE**
■ **WORK** SMART
■ **THINKING AHEAD**

When possible, stack panels on the floor to keep them straight and flat.

straight. Be sure to avoid marring the good face of the panels or damaging the edges. Panels stacked on edge against a wall are easier to measure and cut, but you must keep them from falling over. This can damage the material as well as be a danger to other workers. When I receive a drywall delivery, I like to distribute the panels in neat piles throughout the building to spread out the weight and speed up the hanging process.

Some time ago, my crew and I were drywalling the upstairs ceilings and walls in an old farmhouse. The only room finished upstairs was the master bedroom. Because the stairs were crooked and steep, the only length I was able to maneuver up them was an 8-ft. panel. But I didn't want to use only 8-ft. panels. The walls and ceilings were crooked and patched up, and there was quite a bit of loose plaster; if I'd used all 8-ft. panels, I'd have ended up with a lot of difficult seams. The only way to get longer panels upstairs was through a large window in the finished master bedroom.

Going through a finished room can be a customer's worst nightmare, so to avoid any damage to the master bedroom I covered the room with drop cloths and plastic and removed the window sashes. It took five of us approximately two hours to unload the truck and hand the panels through the window, but it was well worth it in the long run. It sounds like a lot of trouble, but I ended up with a minimum number of seams. As a result, the customer got the best job possible.

If you don't have the luxury of an upper-story access, the drywall's journey upstairs can be a little more circuitous.

Sample House Estimate

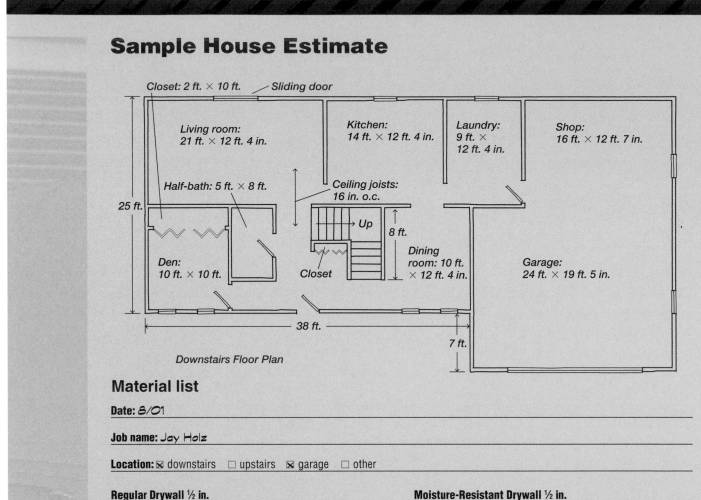

Downstairs Floor Plan

Material list

Date: 8/01

Job name: Jay Holz

Location: ☒ downstairs ☐ upstairs ☒ garage ☐ other

Regular Drywall ½ in.

length		total
8 ft.	☒ ☒	19
10 ft.	☒ ☒ ☒ ☒	36
12 ft.	☒∶	5
14 ft.	☒ ☒∶	15
16 ft.	∶∶	3

Fire-Resistant Drywall   ☒ ⅝ in.   ☐ ½ in.

length		total
8 ft.		
10 ft.	☐	8
12 ft.	☒∶∶	14
14 ft.		

Corner Bead

length	total
8 ft.	
10 ft.	

Moisture-Resistant Drywall ½ in.

length		total
8 ft.	⌶∶	5
10 ft.	∙∙	2
12 ft.		
14 ft.		

Other   Thickness

length		total
8 ft.	∙∙	2
10 ft.	☒∶∶	14
12 ft.		
14 ft.		

Special instructions:

Use 10' panels on end in garage

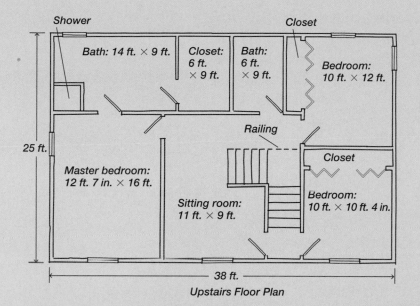

Upstairs Floor Plan

Material list

Date: 8/01

Job name: Jay Holz

Location: ☐ downstairs ☒ upstairs ☐ garage ☐ other

Regular Drywall ½ in.

length		total
8 ft.	☒ ∴	13
10 ft.	☒ ☐	18
12 ft.	☒ ⊔	17
14 ft.	☒ ∴	13
16 ft.	⊔	7

Fire-Resistant Drywall ☐ ⅝ in. ☐ ½ in.

length	total
8 ft.	
10 ft.	
12 ft.	
14 ft.	

Corner Bead

length	total
8 ft.	
10 ft.	

Moisture-Resistant Drywall ½ in.

length		total
8 ft.	·	1
10 ft.	⊔	7
12 ft.	∴	3
14 ft.	∴	3

Other Moisture-Resistant Drywall   Thickness 5/8"

length		total
8 ft.		
10 ft.	⠇	5
12 ft.		
14 ft.		

Special instructions:

Master bedroom (cathedral ceiling):

    use 16' lengths

Bring baker's scaffold

Bathroom ceiling: 5/8" M.R.

Bathroom shower: get (3) 36" X 5' cement boards

    1/2" thick

CHAPTER 2

Tools and Materials

W HEN I STARTED O U T in the drywall business, I could easily carry in my arms all the tools that I needed to hang, tape, and sand a drywalling job. My basic set of tools consisted of a T-square, a utility knife, a screw gun, a prybar, a utility saw, a wooden bench, four trowels, and a hand sander. With these few basic tools, I was limited to relatively simple jobs—drywalling single rooms and small additions, repairing cracks, and doing some minor remodeling—and I had to work pretty hard to get results that I was happy with.

As I gained experience and improved my techniques, I began to take on more challenging jobs, such as drywalling entire houses, working on high ceilings, and hanging drywall on curved surfaces. These more difficult jobs required that I add tools (and manpower) to my drywalling arsenal, including a greater assortment of taping knives, adjustable workbenches, and scaffolding. In addition to using new tools, I have always tried to keep up with the latest developments in drywalling materials. Over the years, the types of fasteners, joint tapes, and joint compounds have changed and new ones have been developed for specific uses.

You can do a pretty good drywalling job with just the basic tools, but you'll get much better results—whether you're a professional or a homeowner—if you have the right materials and equipment.

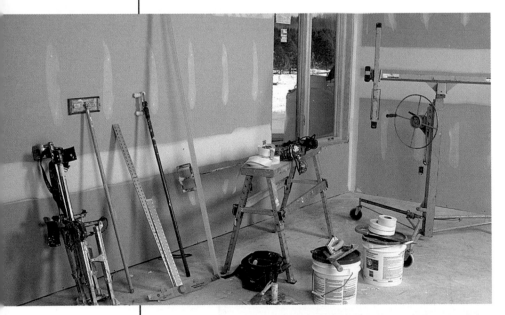

You'll need quite a few tools and materials to work with drywall.

I've organized this chapter roughly in the order in which each tool or material is needed, starting with tools for measuring and marking on through tools for sanding. Rather than listing all the tools first and then listing the materials, I've combined the two categories. For example, you'll find screws and nails with the discussion of screw guns and hammers. I've also included some specialized tools (such as a drywall router, a self-feeding screw gun attachment, and a corner crimper) that can make the job easier or faster. Keep in mind that many of these tools can be rented at a rental equipment store.

Hanging Tools

There are probably more tools required for hanging drywall than for any other step in the process. To do a good job, you'll need an assortment of measuring and marking tools, various cutting tools, tools for lifting and supporting drywall panels, and tools and materials for fastening drywall. Depending on the height of the ceilings, you may also need to use scaffolding.

Measuring and marking tools

Taking accurate measurements is a very important part of drywalling. If you measure a panel too short, you'll have to do some extra patching at the taping stage (see the sidebar on p. 94). If you measure a panel too long and force it into place, the ends will break apart, again requiring additional patching. For accurate measurements, I rely on a 25-ft. tape measure. You'll need a tape that long for calculating materials for large rooms. A 25-ft. tape is a little wider and stiffer than shorter-length tapes, so it extends

A tape measure can be used to scribe short, straight measurements. Pinch the tape at the desired dimension, and then scribe a line with a utility knife as you ride the tape along the edge of the panel.

farther before it bends or sags, which makes it easier to measure long lengths without a helper. Regardless of length, tape measures are also useful for scribing short, straight measurements, as shown in the photo above.

A 4-ft. aluminum T-square, which is used for both marking and cutting drywall, is one tool that you really can't do without. The top edge of the square is butted against the long tapered edge of the drywall panel and the 4-ft. piece hangs down along the face of the panel at 90 degrees (the square can also be used as a straightedge for angled cuts). The edges of the square are calibrated in inches. When marking straight, narrow pieces of drywall, locate the measurement you want on the top edge of the T-square and line it up with the panel edge (see the top left photo on p. 24). Then mark the panel with a pencil or score it with a utility knife. ("Scoring" means cutting through the paper surface of the panel.)

A 24-in. framing square also comes in handy for marking and cutting drywall. I use this square mostly for transferring measurements when cutting out small openings (for electrical boxes, heat-duct openings, and so forth) after a panel has been attached (see the photos on p. 55).

■ WORK SAFE
■ WORK
■ THINKING AHEAD

When marking a straight line for angled cuts, the hook on the end of the chalkline has an annoying habit of slipping off the edge of the panel. If you don't have anyone to hold the hook in place, make a cut about ¼ in. deep at the mark and slide the hooked end of the string into the cut (see the bottom photo on p. 24).

A metal T-square is good for marking narrow strips of drywall and for squaring up the end of a panel. To use it, line up the desired measurement along the top edge of the square.

Use a chalkline in situations when it's difficult to scribe a straight line between two points with a tape measure and a knife or 4-ft. square. Hook the end of the chalkline over the marked point on one end of the panel and stretch the line to the other mark.

A chalkline is used for marking straight lines, primarily ones that are difficult to scribe with a tape measure and a knife or ones that are too long to mark with a 4-ft. square. To mark a line between two points, hook the end of the chalkline over the mark on one end of the panel and stretch the line to the other mark. Pull the line tight, then with your other hand lift the string straight up from the surface a few inches and release it. The colored chalk from the string will leave a mark on the surface.

Similar to a drafting compass, a scriber is used to fit out-of-plumb walls (see the sidebar on the facing page), to mark round openings (see p. 57), and to fit irregular surfaces. When fitting an uneven surface, such as a very wavy ceiling, hold the drywall panel as tightly as possible against the surface, place the metal point of the scriber against the surface at a right angle, and then follow along the contour. As you slide the scriber along the ceiling, the pencil end will leave a mark on the panel. Cut along the pencil line with a utility knife or a saw.

Cutting tools

It's not often that you hang a piece of drywall without having to make some sort of cut. You may need to cut the panel to length or width or make an opening for an electrical outlet box, a

When you are marking an angled line with a chalkline, hook the end of the string into a small notch in the drywall to prevent it from slipping.

Fitting a Square Panel into an Out-of-Plumb Corner

A square-cut panel will not fit properly against a wall that's not plumb. To compensate for the out-of-plumb corner, cut the panel about 1 in. long, and then position it in the corner. Run the point of a scriber (held roughly at a right angle) along the out-of-plumb wall to mark the cutting line, and cut it to fit.

Butt the panel against the corner.

Run the scribes along the out-of-plumb wall to mark the edge of the panel.

After cutting, the panel should fit snugly into the corner.

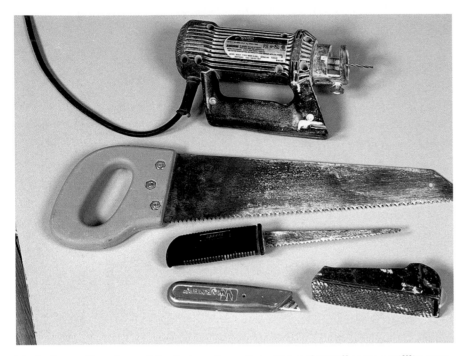

Tools for cutting drywall include a drywall router, a drywall saw, a utility saw, a utility knife, and a rasp.

The most commonly used cutting tool is a utility knife. It is typically used in combination with a 4-ft. square to make cuts across the full width of a panel, though it can be used to cut along the mark left by a chalkline. To cut a panel using a utility knife, follow these steps:

1. Mark the length of the panel, and then cut through the face paper and into the gypsum core (see the left photo below).
2. Snap the panel away from the cut line and make a second cut along the crease on the back of the panel.
3. Snap the panel forward again, so that the two pieces separate cleanly.

The sharper the knife blade and the deeper the cut, the smoother the cut edge will be. If the knife is sharp, one stroke on each side of the panel will be sufficient. A dull blade will create a jagged cut that may leave the panel a little longer than measured (see the right photo below). The jagged edge can be trimmed

window, or a door. On some panels, you may have to make more than one cut. The tools described in this section will help you make clean, accurate cuts in any type of drywall.

To make a cut across the full width of a panel, score the paper with a utility knife along the edge of a T-square.

A dull blade in a utility knife can leave a jagged cut edge.

The author uses a utility knife that has a serrated edge in the handle. Make the cut with the blade and use the handle as a rasp.

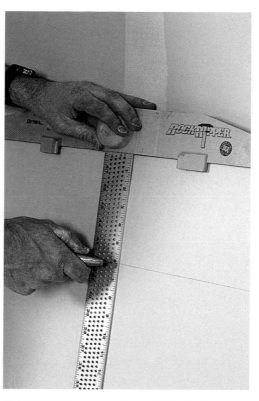

This scribing square has calibrated notches along the blade. To score a panel, insert the knife blade into the proper notch, and then slide the top of the square along the edge of the drywall panel. The result is a quick, clean cut.

off with a utility knife, or for a better job, smoothed out with a drywall rasp. I use a utility knife that has a serrated section built into the handle. After making the cut, I use the rough area as a drywall rasp (see the left photo above).

One type of scribing square lets you score the drywall as you measure. The long edge of the tool has small slots that hold the blade of the knife in place as you slide the top of the square along the edge of the panel (see the right photo above).

SAWS. Customers are sometimes surprised to see me using a saw to cut drywall, but in certain instances it's faster and easier to use than a utility knife. The teeth in drywall saws have more "set" in them than standard woodcutting handsaws. (The set is determined by the amount the teeth are bent out in each direction; the wider the set, the wider the kerf taken out with the saw.) The wide-set teeth rip through the paper and gypsum core quite easily, and the wide kerf also

helps prevent damage to the paper surface when the blade is drawn back.

There are two types of saws for cutting drywall. I use a smaller drywall utility saw to cut openings for electrical outlets, pipes, and ducts and to cut square pieces out of panels. This saw has a sharp pointed end, making it easy to start a cut in the center of a panel. I use a larger drywall saw, which is stiffer than an ordinary woodcutting saw, to cut along a door or window opening after the drywall has been hung over the opening and tacked in place. (Make this cut only if the door or window jambs have not been installed; otherwise, you'll damage the jambs.)

The larger drywall saw also works well for trimming panels that run a little long at the outside corners or at the edge out small openings in drywall panels. A specially designed router bit cuts through the drywall as it follows along the edge of an electrical box or a heat-duct opening. Cutting openings with a router requires less accurate measurements than does cutting with a saw, because you need to find only one edge and follow it around (see p. 54). If you use this tool, be sure to apply only light pressure; if you apply too much pressure, the bit could cut right through a plastic electrical box.

Lifting tools

All drywall panels have to be lifted into place before they are attached. Sometimes they may have to be held only about ½ in. off the floor; other times, they may need to be hoisted to the top of a cathedral ceiling.

When hanging drywall on a wall horizontally (my preferred method of working), the top panel can be lifted into place by hand and nailed or screwed home. The bottom panel is then set into place and lifted up, usually less than 1 in. off the floor, to butt against the bottom of the top panel. You can use a small prybar to hold the panel off the floor, but this tool usually requires using one or both hands. I prefer to use a panel lifter that is operated by foot, leaving both hands free to attach the panel.

On flat ceilings, a T-support is a handy tool for holding a panel in place, freeing up your hands for fastening. This simple prop can be made out of a furring strip or a 2×4 with a 4-ft.-long furring strip screwed to the top. It's best to make the T-support on the job to fit the height of the ceiling (I make mine about ½ in. longer than the ceiling height so it will fit snugly). One option is to buy a T-support like the one shown at the bottom on the facing page. Known as a "stiff arm," this support is made of metal and is adjustable to accommodate different ceiling heights.

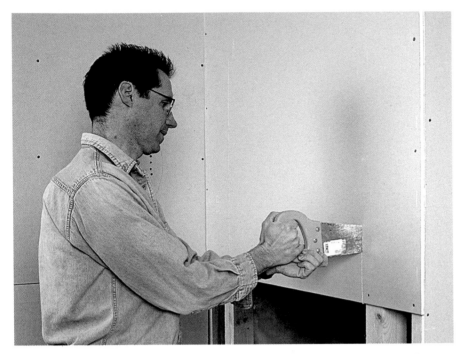

A drywall saw has many uses, one of which is to cut the attached panel along a doorway opening (always cut from the face side to avoid damaging the finish side).

of a doorway. Another use for this rigid saw is to make beveled cuts, which are sometimes necessary for a good fit at corners that are greater than 90 degrees.

DRYWALL ROUTER. A drywall router is a specialized tool that's great for cutting

A drywall router is a specialized tool for cutting out holes for electrical boxes and other small openings. It uses a special bit with a guide tip that follows the outside edge of the opening.

A panel lifter is a handy tool for raising a drywall panel an inch or so off the floor. Controlling the lift with your foot frees up your hands to guide the panel into position.

Hanging drywall is usually a job for two or more people, but a drywall lift (available from rental tool stores) makes it possible for one person to hang drywall alone. The lift adjusts to various heights of walls and ceilings (sloped as well as flat) and to panels of different lengths. The panel is placed finished face toward the lift. For ceilings, begin by roughly positioning the panel, with one end tilted up slightly. Position the panel into its exact place as you crank up the lift, and leave the lift in place until the edges of the drywall are fastened.

Step-up benches or trestles are typically used for reaching ceilings up to 10 ft. high. These stable aluminum benches are about 4 ft. long and 10 in. wide and are adjustable in height from about 18 in. to 32 in. Optional legs bring the bench height up to 48 in. The horizontal supports can be used as a step when climbing onto the bench with a drywall panel (see the right photo on p. 30) or as a support for a short plank stretched between two benches. The bench should be adjusted to a height that places your head close to the ceiling. After the panel is lifted into place, it can be held there with light head pressure, leaving both hands free to attach the panel.

A simple T-support can really help when you need a free pair of hands for fastening.

A modern version of a T-support, called a stiff arm, adjusts to different heights and holds a panel firmly in place with hydraulic pressure.

For ceilings that are too high for benches, a baker's scaffold provides a stable, adjustable platform (see the bottom photo on the facing page). Scaffolds are available in 6-ft., 8-ft., and 10-ft. lengths and are adjustable up to 6 ft. high. Some baker's scaffolds can be stacked two sections high. A single section can be guided through most doorways, so it doesn't need to be disassembled if you want to move it from room to room.

For higher ceilings or walls, a wider stable platform is a must. The scaffold should be at least 4 ft. wide and 10 ft. long, and it should be adjustable at least every 15 in. or so. It should also have horizontal end supports, so that you can run planks at different heights (see the

A drywall lift is a specialized tool for hanging drywall on ceilings and upper walls.

A fully extended bench can be wobbly, but you can purchase an attachment that provides stability and a step at a comfortable height.

Drywall benches provide a stable platform for working on ceilings and upper walls. Some benches are adjustable for added height.

photo at right). Working on any type of scaffolding demands attention to safety; the sidebar below lists some important precautions.

STILTS. I use stilts primarily when I'm taping and sanding, but some pros like to use them when hanging drywall, too. Stilts provide a lot of mobility and eliminate the need for benches and scaffolding on ceilings less than 9 ft. high. They make it easy to apply long lengths of joint tape and to finish an entire seam at one go, thereby helping to increase productivity and the quality of the job. (Note that safety regulations in some states do not allow the use of stilts, and many insurance policies do not cover workers who are injured while working on stilts.)

When I bought my first pair of stilts, it took me a few weeks to summon up the courage to use them. I was afraid I'd make a fool of myself in front of a customer (and in front of my workmates!). But when I finally tried the stilts, it didn't take too long to get the hang of them. It's

A drywall scaffold should be strong and stable and have crossbars at least every 15 in. at the ends.

An adjustable baker's scaffold provides stable support when installing and taping drywall up to heights of 12 ft.

Safety Precautions When Working on Scaffolding

■ The floor supporting any scaffolding should be sound, rigid, and capable of carrying the load without settling or displacement. Any scaffold that is damaged or weakened should be repaired immediately.

■ Scaffolds between 4 ft. and 10 ft. high should have standard guardrails on all open sides and ends of the platform. Guardrails should be made of lumber no smaller than 2×4 and installed 42 in. above the platform surface, with a midrail of 1×6 lumber.

■ Any platform over 10 ft. high should have toeboards as well as guardrails on all open sides and ends. Toeboards should be at least 4 in. high and extend around the perimeter of the platform.

■ Scaffold planks should extend at least 6 in. over the end supports and should be placed with the edges close together.

■ If you are working in an area where there is any risk of head injury, wear an approved hard hat.

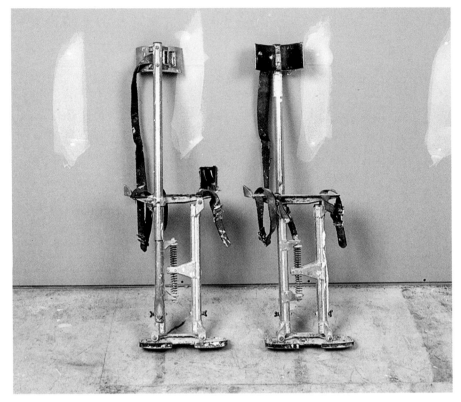

Most stilts are adjustable for different heights. This pair has joints that flex with ankle movement.

so much easier (and faster) to work on stilts than to drag around benches and ladders, and as long as you keep all work areas clean, using stilts is probably safer, too. Now I use stilts not only for taping and sanding but also for insulating ceilings and for cutting in with a paintbrush along ceiling edges.

Fastening tools and materials

Drywall can be hung with nails or screws. If you use nails, you'll need a drywall hammer, which looks a little like a hatchet. The blade end is tapered (but not sharp), so it can be used for prying or lifting. The hammer has a convex face, which leaves a shallow dimple in the front of the drywall without tearing the face paper (a standard carpenter's hammer has a flat face, which can easily tear the paper). The dimple is concealed with joint compound during the taping process.

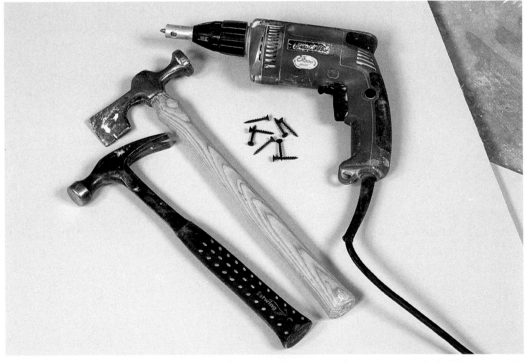

A drywall screw gun and a drywall hammer are the best tools for fastening panels. To minimize the risk of tearing the face paper, use a convex-faced drywall hammer (center) rather than a standard flat-faced carpenter's hammer (left).

A cordless, self-feeding screw gun saves a lot of time and energy when attaching panels.

A self-feeding attachment can be purchased to fit most any screw gun.

Nowadays, most professional dry-wallers use screws rather than nails, and the drywall screw gun has replaced the hammer as the tool of choice for attaching panels. A screw gun installs a screw with a bugle head just below the surface of the drywall paper. The nose of the screw gun pushes the drywall panel against the framing as the screw is installed. It has a positive clutch that is engaged when pressure is applied to the Phillips bit. The depth of the screw bit can be modified; when properly adjusted, the screw gun sets the screw just below the surface without tearing the face paper. Both corded and cordless models are available.

Fastener Specifications

Fastener Type	Drywall Thickness	Minimum Fastener Length
Wood screws (coarse thread)	⅜ in., ½ in., ⅝ in.	1 in., 1⅛ in., 1¼ in.
Screws into metal studs or furring (fine thread)	⅜ in., ½ in., ⅝ in.	¾ in., ⅞ in., 1 in.
Ring-shank nails (wood studs only)	⅜ in., ½ in., ⅝ in.	1⅛ in., 1¼ in., 1⅜ in.

Screwing is faster than nailing, but having to place every screw onto the bit by hand is time-consuming (and tedious). A self-feeding screw gun solves that problem. Or you can buy a self-feeding attachment for your current screw gun. A string of screws feeds into the nosepiece as each screw is used, greatly increasing productivity. Self-feeding screw gun attachments are available to fit most brands; they accept screws from 1 in. to 1¾ in. long.

SCREWS AND NAILS. Fastening drywall with screws is preferred over nailing, because screws are faster to install than nails, they do less damage to the drywall panel, and they hold the drywall tighter against the framing. Screws for wood framing should be long enough to penetrate the framing at least ⅝ in. (see the chart above). Screws for light-gauge metal framing have finer threads than wood framing screws; they should penetrate at least ⅜ in. Use self-tapping screws for heavier gauge metal. (Note that you should always use screws in metal studs—nails will not hold.)

If you do use nails, they should penetrate the wood framing at least ¾ in. Ring-shank nails are preferred over plain-shank nails because they have 25 percent greater holding power. (The holding power is greatly diminished if the drywall face is damaged, so be careful not to tear the paper or sink the nail

■ WORK SAFE
■ WORK SMART
■ THINKING AHEAD

No matter which type of fastener you use, be sure the panel is tight against the framing and that the fasteners are properly set. Always use the recommended length fastener.

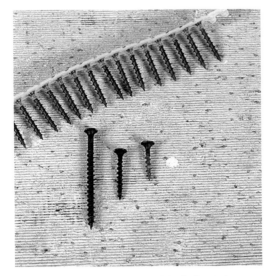

Drywall screws are available in lengths starting at 1 in. and are sold either loose or collated for self-feeding screw guns.

Screws for attaching drywall to metal framing feature a fine thread and often have a drill-point tip for easy penetration of the metal.

Coarse-thread screws are used for wood framing; fine-thread screws are used for metal framing.

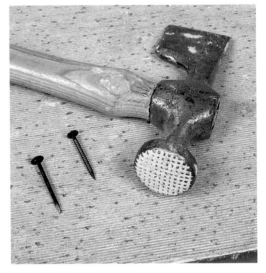

Ring-shank drywall nails, such as the one on the right, have 25 percent more holding power than the smooth shank nail on the left.

too deep, which can severely damage the gypsum core.)

Outside corner beads

Whether on a wall or on a soffit, outside corners must be covered with corner bead. The material protects the surface and has a slightly raised beaded edge, which keeps the corner straight and acts as a screed while taping.

It wasn't too long ago that square-edged metal corner bead was the only product available. Today, you have your choice of metal, vinyl, plastic covered with paper, or metal covered with paper. Some types are available in 100-ft. rolls. Bullnose bead is also available. There are a lot of great products on the market that offer protection, provide a variety of design options, and make application easier.

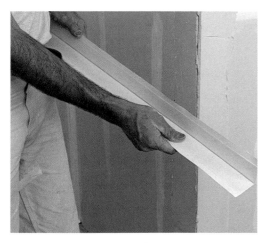

There are many types of corner beads available. This one is a paper-covered plastic outside corner bead that is attached with joint compound.

The corner bead attached. The bead protects vulnerable areas and makes taping easier.

Installation techniques vary from product to product. You can nail or screw metal bead in place or you can use a corner crimper. This device crimps the flat edges of the bead into the drywall, holding it in place. Other types of corner bead are embedded in drywall compound or glued onto the panels. All corner beads should be installed in one piece, unless the length of the corner exceeds the standard corner bead lengths of 6 ft. 10 in., 8 ft., 9 ft., and 10 ft. See chapters 3 and 4 for more on installing corner beads.

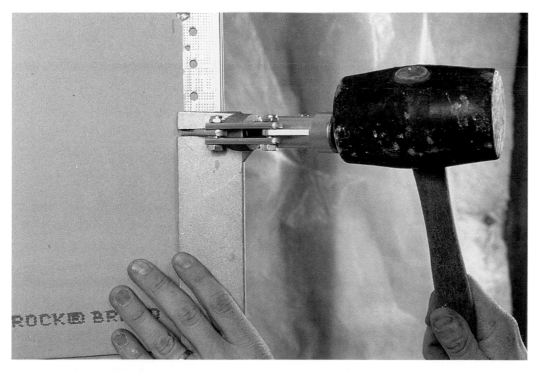

One blow with a rubber mallet on a corner crimper every 4 to 6 in. attaches standard metal corner bead to an outside corner.

Metal Corner Bead

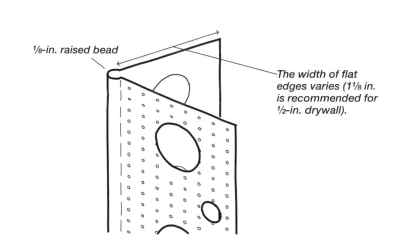

⅛-in. raised bead

The width of flat edges varies (1⅛ in. is recommended for ½-in. drywall).

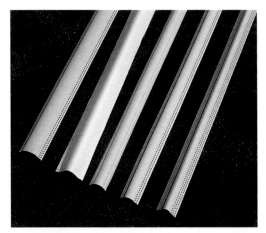

Bullnose corner beads are quite popular, because they provide an easy way to add an elegant look to a room. They are available in many materials and radii, ranging from ⅜ in. to 1½ in.

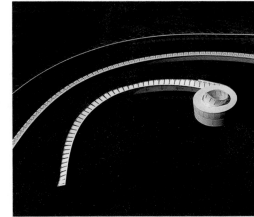

These flexible archway beads are also available in bullnose form.

ARCHWAY BEAD. For years, I used metal corner bead to finish the edges of archways. The only way to install it was to snip the bead at 1-in. intervals and push each piece into place along the curve of the arch. This method worked, but it cannot be compared to the simplicity and quality you get with new products made specifically for archways. There are three basic types of flexible corner bead made for arches:

■ Flexible wire bead has a plastic beaded edge and is nailed in place.
■ Vinyl bead has a pre-snipped edge that is glued and stapled in place.
■ Composite bead has a PVC core and a paper surface and is embedded in joint compound.

The PVC material comes in a roll. The wire and vinyl beads come in lengths of up to 10 ft. and the composite bead comes in lengths of up to 100 ft. Vinyl bullnose corner bead, which is flexible, is available to match the outside and inside corner bullnose beads. Everyone has his or her favorites. I've had good success with the vinyl beads.

Inside corner beads

On most inside corners, I use paper tape embedded in joint compound and feathered to a smooth edge. This method works great for perfectly square, 90-degree corners, but it is the off-angle corner—the one that isn't a perfect 90 degrees—that requires a specialized product. Fortunately, there are a number of products that can handle these off angles.

The first is a flexible metal bead covered with paper. It makes taping off-angle inside and outside corners a breeze.

There are a number of products available. Some work on both inside and outside corners; others are more specialized and designed for application on specific-

Special tapes for inside corners provide excellent and long-lasting results. The one on top has a flexible center.

angle corners. For off-angle inside corners, there is even a product that has a rubber center groove, which flexes if the structure moves slightly, greatly reducing costly callbacks. Inside corner beads are also available in bullnose styles to match bullnose outside corners. These products cost a little more than paper-type corner beads and compound, but you easily make up the extra cost in time saved.

Trim beads

Metal, plastic, and paper-covered metal J-trims are caps used to cover the edges of drywall panels. Typically, they are applied against a shower stall, a window jamb, or a brick wall; around an opening that is left untrimmed; or on the exposed end of a panel. J-trim is available in different thicknesses to fit different sizes of drywall. It can be installed

before the panel is hung or after the panel is loosely attached. It is held in place by driving a nail or screw through the face of the drywall and through the longer back flange of the J-trim. Some types need to be finished with joint compound and some do not require finishing (see the drawing on p. 38).

An L-bead finishes the edges of drywall that butt up against something, such as a suspended ceiling, a window, or a paneled wall. The drywall is cut so the short edge of the L-bead can be inserted between the drywall and the other material. The exposed edge of the bead is finished with joint compound. Many of these L-beads have a removable strip that protects the abutting surface from compound and paint. Trim beads are available in lengths of up to 12 ft. long and for ½-in.- and ⅝-in.-thick drywall.

> ■ **WORK SAFE**
> ■ **WORK**
> ■ **THINKING AHEAD**
>
> **For off-angle corners, use a flexible metal bead covered with paper. It does a good job of keeping those types of corners straight.**

J-Trim and L-Bead

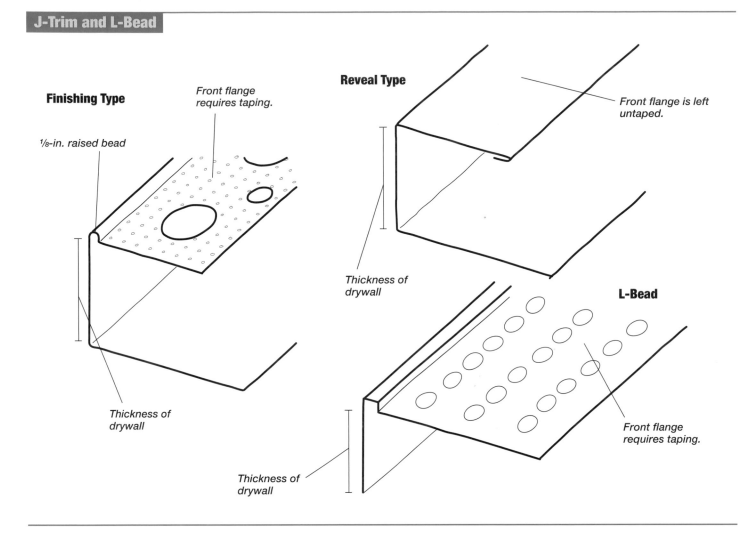

Finishing Type

⅛-in. raised bead

Front flange
requires taping.

Thickness of
drywall

Reveal Type

Front flange is left
untaped.

Thickness of
drywall

L-Bead

Front flange
requires taping.

Thickness of
drywall

Expansion joints

Expansion joints, which are made of
metal or vinyl, are installed between drywall panels. They are not covered with
joint compound, as other typical drywall
joints are, but they can be filled with a
flexible caulk. Expansion joints are
designed to compensate for the expansion and contraction of building materials and for the normal settling of a
building, so that drywall seams don't
become cracked or ridged. They are used
when there is a large expanse of ceiling or
wall. On ceilings, they run from wall to
wall; on walls, they run from ceiling to
floor. In high stairway walls, they are
installed from wall to wall.

Taping Tools
and Materials

It used to be that a couple of trowels, a
roll of paper tape, and a pail of joint compound were all that you needed to do a
typical taping job. Nowadays, there are
many types and sizes of trowels, various
options for reinforcing seams, and so
many different kinds of joint compounds
that you may not know where to begin
when deciding which one to use.

Trowels

There are four types of trowels that I use
for taping, all of which are available in
different sizes for different applications.

As I discuss each trowel, I'll mention the size that I use most often and, where appropriate, explain what features to look for when purchasing a trowel. I'll explain how to use each trowel in greater detail in chapter 4.

TAPING KNIVES, which are available in widths from 1 in. to 6 in. (in 1-in. increments), are used for taping seams and corners and covering fasteners. The wider widths often have a metal end on the handle for resetting nail heads. Narrower widths come in handy for taping tight areas (for example, the often-narrow space between a doorframe and a corner). I use a 6-in. knife more than any other size. Whatever the width of the knife, it should be fairly stiff and have some "give" but not be too flexible. Cheaper, flimsier trowels are harder to work with and tend to leave too much joint compound on the surface. Stiffer knives give you more control and are less prone to bending and nicks in the blade.

When buying a taping knife, look for one that has a little curve in the blade when viewed from head on. If you can't find one, you can put a slight curve in the blade by bending it over a rounded surface, such as a pipe. I use the convex side of the blade when taping. Because the curve helps keep the corners of the blade slightly away from the taping surface, the result is a smooth surface without the ridges created by a flat knife blade.

A square-cornered taping knife cannot reach into a corner very well if the corner is less than 90 degrees (for example, at the intersection of a sloped ceiling and a wall or at the top of a cellar stairway). In these areas, I use a pointed trowel, which can easily be made by cutting off the sides of an old 6-in. taping knife. A small pointed mason's trowel also works well for this purpose.

A quality hand-taping job depends on a variety of taping tools.

A hawk is used to hold large amounts of joint compound when taping with a knife or trowel.

A beveled (curved) trowel has a slight curve in the blade to better feather and finish the seams.

HAWKS are used to hold large quantities of joint compound when working with a taping knife. These tools have a square aluminum top with circular grooves to help prevent the joint compound from sliding off, and a short, straight handle centered on the underside. Hawks are available in sizes from 8 in. to 14 in. square. I prefer to work with the largest size.

CURVED OR BEVELED TROWELS have a slight curve in the blade that is about $\frac{5}{32}$ in. deep. They are available in lengths

from 10 in. to 14 in. and in widths of 4 in. and 4½ in. I prefer to use a curved trowel rather than a flat trowel, because the curve helps finish seams in an inconspicuous crown.

I use the 4½-in. by 14-in. curved trowel for feathering and finishing most seams, as well as for holding joint compound while applying it with a taping knife. It has many uses, and I always

Trowel Care

■ While working, keep trowels free of dry joint compound to avoid marks or scratches when trying to smooth the compound. Use another trowel (or the edge of the hawk) to scrape off any excess compound. When you've finished a taping session, clean trowels with warm water.

■ Use trowels for taping only. Don't scrape floors or apply adhesive or tile grout with your taping tools.

■ Protect edges from nicks or scratches; any nicks should be sanded or filed smooth.

■ Round any sharp corners on a new trowel with a file (sharp corners can rip the joint tape).

Adjustable off-angle knives are handy for finishing off-angle inside corners with paper tape.

seem to have a curved trowel and a 6-in. taping knife in my hand while taping.

WIDE STRAIGHT-HANDLED TAPING KNIVES are much the same as narrow taping knives, except they have a metal reinforcing strip at the back of the blade. I don't use them for embedding tape. Rather, I use them for applying and smoothing out the final thin finish coats of joint compound on seams and outside corners, as well as for smoothing out large areas and seam intersections. Straight-handled taping knives are available in widths from 10 in. to 24 in. As with regular taping knifes, they should have a slight curve in the blade and the corners should be rounded with a file. I use a 12-in. knife for most applications.

Mechanical taping tools

These tools are quite popular today because they cut down on labor. There are mechanical tools available for each step in the taping process. Mechanical taping tools are expensive, but you can rent them. They are used mainly for larger jobs, but sometimes I use them when I'm working on two or three smaller jobs at once.

Joint tape

Joint tape is used to reinforce seams and corners and to repair cracks and holes in drywall and plaster. There are two types of tape: pre-creased paper tape and fiberglass-mesh tape.

PAPER TAPE. Not long ago, paper tape was the only tape you could buy. It is still widely used and is a good all-around tape for seams, cracks, and small holes. Available in rolls 2 in. wide and 250 ft. to 500 ft. long, paper tape has a light crease down the center, which helps it fold easily for use on inside corners. Although mesh tape has largely supplanted paper

Wider taping knives are very useful during the taping process.

tape for finishing tapered edge seams, paper tape still has a number of advantages and uses.

- It is stronger than mesh and not as likely to be torn by taping tools.
- It resists stretching and wrinkling more effectively than mesh tape does.

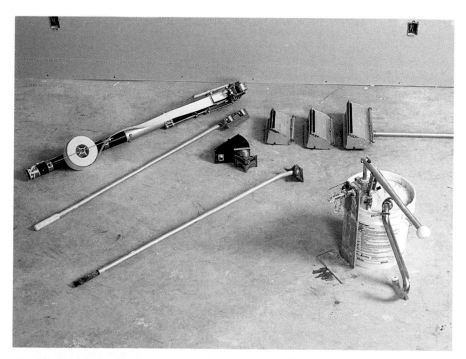

As an alternative to hand taping, you can buy or rent a variety of mechanical taping tools. An automatic taper is shown at top left. The three boxes to the right are used to apply different widths of joint compound.

Pre-creased paper tape is the strongest tape. The crease also makes it easy to use on inside corners.

Fiberglass self-adhesive mesh tape is fool-proof for taping seams and small patches.

- It works much better than mesh for taping inside corners, as the crease makes it easier to keep the tape centered and straight.
- It is cheaper than mesh.

On the downside, paper tape is more time consuming to apply (it has to be embedded in a coat of compound) and is prone to bubbling if you don't apply enough compound.

FIBERGLASS-MESH TAPE. This tape is commonly used for taping tapered seams and for patching cracks and small holes. It is also used to reinforce gaps between panels or corners that are more than ¼ in. wide. Mesh tape can be used on regular inside corners, but it is hard to keep centered and straight. In addition, it is easy to cut through with a taping knife when finishing corners (or to sand through in areas where only a thin layer of compound has been applied).

Fiberglass-mesh tape comes in rolls that are 1½ in. or 2 in. wide and 300 ft. or 500 ft. long. There are two types: self-adhesive tape, which is simply pressed in place over a seam, and nonadhesive (or plain) tape. In addition, there are two types of self-adhesive mesh tapes. One is traditional leno-weave mesh, which, when used with a drying-type joint compound, is subject to cracking and stretching when a joint is under stress. The other is a newer tape with a cross-fiber design that adds strength and crack resistance to joints. Nonadhesive tape is less expensive but not as easy to work with as the self-adhesive varieties (it has to be stapled in place over a seam). All types of mesh tape can be cut with a utility knife or the sharp edge of a trowel.

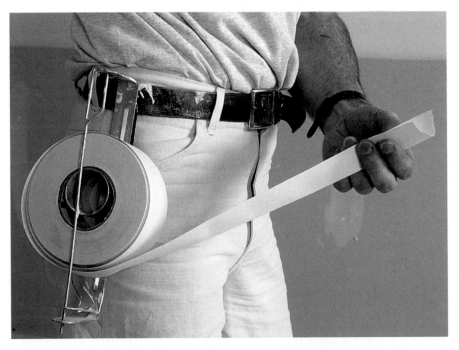

A tape holder is a handy dispenser for paper or mesh tape.

If you're taping a lot of seams, a handy tool to have at your side is a tape reel (also known as a tape holder). The reel, which attaches to your belt, can hold up to a 500-ft. roll and works with both paper and mesh tapes. The tape rolls off the reel for quick and easy tear off.

Joint compound

There are so many types and brands of joint compound that it can be difficult to know which ones to use. The most important distinction is between drying-type compounds and setting-type compounds. In this section, I'll describe some of the most popular types within each of these categories.

DRYING-TYPE JOINT COMPOUND is the more common type—it's the type you see in buckets at your local hardware store. It is available in premixed and powdered forms. Premixed drying-type joint compound comes in 1-gal. and 5-gal. buckets and boxes. The 1-gal. size is good for patching small jobs; the 5-gal. bucket is enough to tape an average 12-ft. by 12-ft. room.

The main advantage of premixed compound is that it is ready to use right out of the bucket. The consistency of the mix is factory controlled, and most brands are equal in quality. Also, there is little waste with premixed compound—the bucket can be resealed and used again later. When using premixed compound, the fresher the better. Keep buckets out of direct sunlight and never allow the compound to freeze. Premixed compound will not keep indefinitely, especially after it has been opened; at room temperature, an open bucket of compound will start to go bad in about a month.

Powdered drying-type joint compound has all the same working characteristics as premixed compound. The major difference is that it comes in dry form and must be mixed with water. Drying-type compound can be stored at any temperature for extended periods (though it should always be warmed to room temperature before mixing).

I use three kinds of drying-type joint compound on a regular basis: taping compound, topping compound, and all-purpose joint compound (each is available premixed or dry).

■ Taping compound is used to embed the joint tape for the first coat and as filler for the second coat (see chapter 4). It is a strong compound, has little shrinkage as it dries, and has excellent bonding and resistance to cracking.

A wide range of joint compounds is available. Always match the compound to the job at hand.

Choosing the Right Joint Compound

When deciding which type of joint compound to use, consider the following factors:

■ The size of the job (for a small job, it is less convenient to use two or three types of compound).

■ The drying and heating conditions (temperature, airflow, and humidity).

■ The availability of materials, including water, at the job site. Taping compound and some of the fast-drying setting-type compounds are available only at larger drywall-supply stores.

■ The amount of time you have to complete the job (use setting-type compounds if time is short).

■ The recommended combination of products (for example, mesh tape should be embedded in a taping compound or in a setting-type compound).

■ Personal preferences (such as the convenience of the premixed drying type versus the strength and better bonding of the setting type).

■ WORK SAFE ■ WORK ■ THINKING AHEAD

Be aware that setting time can be adversely affected by overmixing or undermixing, mixing too thick or too thin, or using dirty water and equipment.

■ Topping compound is used for a thin finishing coat. It is easy to work with, feathers out nicely, dries quickly, and sands smooth. Topping compound can be used over taping compound or over all-purpose joint compound.

■ As its name suggests, all-purpose compound can be used for all stages of the taping process—as an embedment for the tape, as a filler coat, and as a finish coat. Because it's more convenient to deal with just one type, all-purpose compound is the most commonly used compound. However, it doesn't have the same strength, bonding qualities, or stability as the taping and topping combination.

All drying-type compounds require an application temperature of at least 55°F (this includes air, surface, and compound temperatures). The compound must dry thoroughly between coats, and the drying time is greatly affected by temperature, humidity, and airflow. Under good conditions, drying-type compounds dry within 24 hours.

SETTING-TYPE JOINT COMPOUND. While drying-type compounds are vinyl-based and dry as the water evaporates, setting-type compounds harden by chemical reaction. The great advantage of setting-type compounds, which are usually available in powdered form, is that they harden faster than drying-type compounds. Unlike drying-type compounds, setting-type compounds actually harden before the joint is completely dry. When first mixed, setting compound is smooth and as easy to use as drying compound. But as it sets, the compound stiffens and becomes difficult to work with.

Setting times vary from 20 minutes to 6 hours, depending on the type used. I prefer a product that sets in 3 to 4 hours, which gives me enough time to apply the compound to the seams. I know that it will be ready for another coat of compound by the next day, even in humid or cool conditions (air, surface, and compound temperatures can be as low as 45°F). Furthermore, setting compound can be given a second and third coat as soon as it sets up—you don't have to wait until it is completely dry. Other benefits include better bonding qualities, less shrinkage and cracking, and a harder finish.

Given that setting-type compounds have so many advantages, you may wonder why anyone would use anything else. But there is a downside: The stuff is much harder to sand, which means that you have to get it as smooth as possible while taping. (However, there is a lightweight setting-type compound that is easier to sand than the stronger, standard type compound, either an all-purpose compound or a topping one.

There is also a relatively new premixed compound that acts as either a setting type or a drying type. The product comes with an additive that you mix into the compound—no need to bring fresh water to the job site. When you use the additive, you create a setting-type compound. Without the additive, the material is used as a drying compound.

Mixing tools

Joint compound can be mixed with a powered paddle or by hand (see the top photo on p. 46 and the discussion on pp. 81-83). For thorough mixing and textured finishes, use a mixing paddle with a

A premixed setting compound is something I always keep in stock. It can be used as a regular compound or mixed with an accelerator to create a setting compound with a desired setting time.

type.) Also, you should mix only as much compound as you can use before it sets up. Unlike powdered drying-type compound, it cannot be stored and reused at a later date.

For much of my work, I like to use a setting-type compound to embed the tape (first coat). I'll often use the same type of compound for the second, filler coat, making sure to take the time to get the compound as smooth as possible. For the third and final coat, I use a drying-

■ **WORK SAFE**
■ **WORK**
■ **THINKING AHEAD**

Use a drying-type compound, which is easier to sand, for the final coat, no matter which type of compound you used for the first two coats.

Approximate Coverage of Materials

Screws and Nails

The number of fasteners used to attach drywall depends on framing spacing, fastener spacing, panel length, and panel orientation. For rough estimating, I usually figure around 1,000 fasteners per 1,000 sq. ft. of drywall.

Joint Tape

It usually takes about 370 lin. ft. of joint tape to finish 1,000 sq. ft. of drywall.

Joint compound

The amounts figured below are estimates for a complete taping job (three coats):

■ Premixed drying-type joint compound: 11 gal. per 1,000 sq. ft. of drywall.

■ Powdered drying-type compound: 80 lb. mixed with water per 1,000 sq. ft. of drywall. (Powdered compound is usually sold in 25-lb. bags.)

■ Setting-type joint compounds vary in weight by types. A rough guide is to figure about 3 bags of setting compound per 1,000 sq. ft. of drywall.

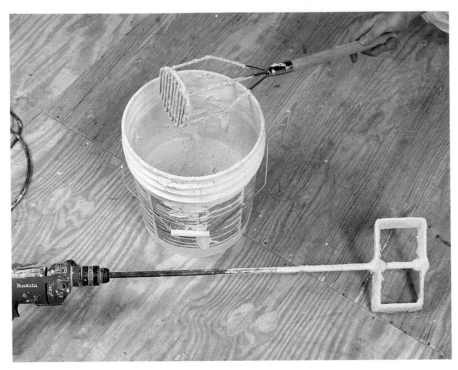

Joint compound can be mixed with a powered mixing paddle or with a hand mixer.

Tools for sanding drywall include a hand sander, a triangle-shaped sander, a pole sander, a sanding sponge, and a folded piece of sandpaper.

heavy-duty ½-in. electric drill. You can use a hand mixer for ready-mixed compounds that have sat too long or been thinned with water for easier application.

Sanding Tools and Materials

Sanding is the final stage in the drywalling process. You can sand joint compound with a piece of folded sandpaper; however, there are a number of tools that help make this unpleasant (but important) task a little more efficient.

Sanders

I use a pole sander for most sanding work. It has a pivoting head designed to hold precut sanding screens or drywall sandpaper. The 4-ft.-long handle helps you reach along the top edge of a wall or near the floor without having to stretch or bend too much. Most low ceilings can also be reached with a pole sander. Grasp the handle with both hands for better leverage.

For areas that are easy to reach or that are too tight for a pole sander, a hand sander is a good alternative. It's the same size as a pole sander (with a 4 in. by 8 in. head) but without the pole. In addition, I recently purchased a triangular sander with a replaceable sandpaper pad that I use as a hand sander or as an attachment for a pole sander. Its pointed shape and beveled edges allow me to get into tight spaces that nothing other than folded sandpaper can reach.

For the extra-fine sanding work that is necessary after sanding with a pole or a hand sander, I like to use a dry sanding sponge. The small, dense sponge, which is 1 in. thick and coated with grit, is available in sizes ranging from 3 in. by 4 in. to 4 in. by 8 in. Dry sanding sponges are available in fine, medium, and coarse grit; I prefer the fine grit for touch-up sanding. Don't confuse this sanding sponge with the drywall sponge that is used wet.

To get into tight spots that even a sanding sponge can't reach, use a folded piece of sandpaper. Sandpaper allows the best control of any sanding method and works especially well for touching up inside corners.

For jobs where clouds of dust are unacceptable, a wet drywall sponge is the answer. The sponge shown in the top photo at right is a high-density polyurethane sponge that is soft and nonabrasive. These sponges are good for blending the edges of taped areas and for smoothing small defects, but they are not as effective for sanding ridges or built-up areas. You can also use an all-purpose household sponge or even a smooth, soft cloth for wet sanding small areas. However, if you intend to finish-sand with a wet sponge, you really must do a good taping job.

Sanding materials

You can sand joint compound with regular sandpaper, but sanding materials specifically made for drywall are more effective. (The problem with regular sandpaper is that the fine, dusty white powder quickly fills up the grit of the paper, making it ineffective.) Drywall-specific sanding materials usually come precut to fit drywall sanding tools.

Drywall sandpaper, which has a paper back and a black carbide-grit surface, is available in 80 to 220 grit. The higher the grit number, the finer the sandpaper (and the smoother the finish). The 220 grit provides the smoothest finish, but it takes longer to sand down high areas or ridges. A good, universal sandpaper is the 120 grit. The only time I use the 80 or 100 grit is for rough sanding between second and third coats of joint compound (see chapter 4).

Sanding screens, sometimes referred to as sanding cloths, are an alternative to sandpaper. Both sides of the screen are covered with carbide-grit-coated fiberglass mesh. When one side gets dull, the screen can be turned over and used again. Because of the holes in the screen, dust buildup is seldom a problem.

Sanding screens are available in grits from 120 to 200. The 120 grit is a good all-around screen; 150 and finer grits work well for finish sanding. Sanding screens are usually more expensive than sandpaper, but you get more life out of them. Also, a screen cuts through joint compound faster than sandpaper does.

A wet sanding sponge cuts down on the amount of dust produced during the sanding process.

Cartridge sandpaper, a sanding screen, and a sanding pad can be purchased precut to fit pole and hand sanders.

CHAPTER 3

Hanging Drywall

HANGING DRYWALL has the reputation of being a difficult, strenuous job; if done improperly, it certainly can be. But with the right attitude and the right techniques, it's not a job you need approach with trepidation. A job can be as simple as covering a short partition wall or as difficult as hanging a 24-ft.-high cathedral ceiling. However big the job, hanging drywall is more than just cutting a panel and nailing it in place. Joints have to fit properly and be kept to a minimum. Holes for electrical boxes and other openings have to be cut out accurately. Fasteners have to be properly placed and properly set.

Hanging drywall sure is fun.

Straightening a Bowed Stud

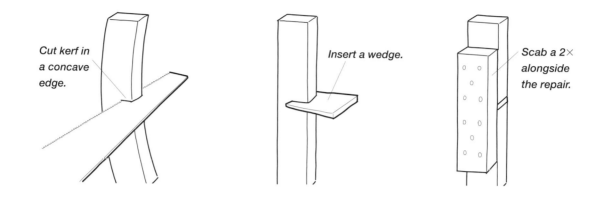

Cut kerf in a concave edge.

Insert a wedge.

Scab a 2× alongside the repair.

A good hanging job provides the foundation for a quality taping job. When I hear someone say that there's no need to be fussy because the tapers can fix it, I know that the finished job will suffer. A good hanger understands the taping process and has respect for the taper.

Drywall panels can be attached in a single layer or in multiple layers. In this chapter, I'll deal with single-layer applications, though most of the procedures are the same for hanging two or more layers. Multilayer applications will be discussed in detail in chapter 6.

Backing Materials

For a quality finish, drywall must be attached to a flat, stable surface. There's not much structural strength in drywall, so if the framing or backing is of poor quality or is weak, the drywall will probably crack or come loose. Drywall can be attached over most surfaces, but it's most commonly applied over wood or metal framing (see the sidebar on p. 68).

Wood framing

When installing drywall over wood framing, make sure that the framing members are aligned in a straight plane. A visual inspection is usually enough to detect badly bowed or twisted studs, though you can hold a straightedge across the studs, if you prefer. If a framing member is bowed or twisted more than ¼ in., it should be straightened or replaced. Renailing sometimes straightens out twisted framing.

A bowed ceiling joist may have to be replaced, but a bowed stud can be straightened by sawing a partial kerf from the concave side. Drive a wedge into the kerfed side, and then nail a 2-ft. or longer stud alongside the existing stud to strengthen it and keep it straight (see the drawing above). Wavy or irregular ceilings can be straightened with 1×1 furring strips nailed across the joists (see the discussion on p. 65). Make minor adjustments with shims driven between the joists and the furring.

It's very important that the framing lumber be dry. If you're working in a cold climate, make sure the framing has been in a heated environment long enough to get the dampness out of the wood. I learned this lesson the hard way on a house in upstate New York that I drywalled and taped in early spring. The owners were very anxious to move in, so we were encouraged to get the job done in a hurry. Most of the house had been framed in the winter and had been exposed to a lot of snow and rain. When I started hanging drywall in the spring, the weather was getting warmer and the house looked dry. I brought in propane heaters to help keep the temperature above 55°F at night in preparation for taping. Everything went well, and the house looked fine when we finished. Later that summer, I got a call from an irate owner, complaining about cracks and buckles in the drywall and peeling tape. As the lumber in the house had dried out, it shrank, twisted, and settled. As the framing settled, the drywall buckled and cracked.

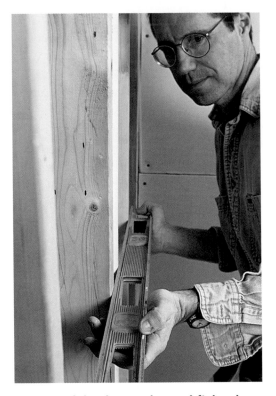

Use a straightedge, such as a 4-ft. level, to check framing that you suspect is out of line.

Drywall-Hanging Weather

The perfect weather for hanging drywall is about 55° to 70°F and relatively dry. The framing lumber should have a moisture content of 15 percent or less. Good luck finding those conditions on a new construction site! For a successful job, you need to create good conditions for application. Here's how:

- Wait as long as possible after the building has been closed in before drywalling.
- Create conditions that will be similar to those of the completed building.
- Bring in heaters to keep the temperature between 55° and 70°F. Keep the heat on 24 hours a day, 7 days a week, until the permanent heating system is working.
- Provide ventilation to remove excess moisture.
- Avoid creating abnormally high or low humidity.

Weather conditions affect the structure, which in turn affects the drywalling job.

Solid backing

On remodeling jobs, I often attach drywall directly over old plaster or paneling. If you're drywalling over a solid backing, be sure to use long enough fasteners that provide a firm attachment to the framing. Drywall can also be hung over rigid urethane insulation. On ceilings with rigid insulation, add 1×1 furring strips before attaching drywall. From experience, I know that the insulation can expand just a little over time, especially with the high temperatures that are common in attics or ceiling cavities. Expanding insulation will cause the fasteners to dimple slightly—they'll probably still be tight, but they will need to be recoated with joint compound.

Measuring and Cutting Drywall

Once you're sure that the backing material is sound, you can begin taking some measurements for the first sheet of drywall. When measuring the length of a wall or ceiling before cutting a drywall

Use a 24-in. framing square to check corners for square.

Cutting a panel to fit too tightly and forcing it into place can cause the edge to break apart. Cut off the broken section with a utility knife.

panel, I usually take two measurements—one where each edge of the panel will be. If the measurements are close, I'll usually use the smaller measurement. If there's quite a difference, say ⅝ in. or more, I'll use both measurements and cut the panel out of square on one or both ends. If the panel must be cut out of square, you need to figure out which end to cut. Check for square by placing a 24-in. framing square in each corner, as shown in the photo above.

Drywall panels should be cut to length, so that they fit loosely into place. A good rule is to cut the panels about ¼ in. short. On ceilings, split the ¼ in. on each end. On walls, always keep the panel edge tight against the panel that is already hung. Never cut the length so the panel is tight and must be forced into place. The ends will break apart and will need to be repaired during taping. Angled walls, such as gable end walls, require careful measurements and cuts (see p. 72).

(see p. 72).

> ■ **WORK SAFE**
> ■ **WORK SMART**
> ■ **THINKING**
>
> Don't force panels into corners, or the edges will crumble and you will have to repair them later.

1. Use a sharp utility knife to score the panel along the edge of a T-square or, for longer or angled cuts, along a marked line.

2. Snap the section of drywall away from the cut side.

3. Score along the crease on the back.

4. Snap the piece forward for a clean break.

Cutting panels

Cutting drywall is probably the easiest part of the whole job. When cutting with a utility knife, use the "score and snap" method (see the photos on the facing page). Run the utility knife along the edge, using enough pressure to cut through the paper and just into the gypsum core. One pass of the knife should be sufficient, as long as you're using a sharp blade. Snap the panel away from the cut, and then cut the back paper with the knife. Snap the panel forward to separate the two pieces.

When using a utility knife, it doesn't matter whether you cut the face or the back of the panel first. I prefer to score each panel on the face side first, but since the panels are packaged face to face in pairs, I cut every other panel from the back. When cutting from the back, be very careful not to tear the face paper on the second pass. Always snap the panel away from you for a clean cut. If the cut is a little ragged or you've cut the panel a little long, use a drywall rasp for smoothing and light shaping.

When cutting drywall with a drywall utility saw or a drywall saw (see p. 26), always cut from the face side of the panel to avoid damaging the finish paper as you push the blade through. The saw cuts on the forward stroke but, as you pull the saw back, be careful not to rip the face paper. (The saw teeth will damage the back paper slightly on the forward stroke, but this is not a cause for concern.)

Cutting holes for large openings

If the doors and windows are not yet installed, you can hang the drywall right over the openings before cutting them out. With the panel installed, cut along each side of the opening with a drywall saw. Score along the top of the opening on the back of the panel, snap the panel

Smooth jagged edges with a rasp. Here the author is using a utility knife with a rasping edge.

forward, and cut off the waste with a utility knife.

If the doors and windows have already been installed, measure and cut out the opening before hanging the drywall. Mark the opening on the face side of the panel and cut it out with a drywall saw. If the window is installed but not the window jambs, you can attach the panel before you cut out the opening. Just follow each side of the window's rough opening with a saw. The top of the window opening can also be cut with a saw, but it's easier to use a utility knife to score the height of the window opening on the back of the panel before attaching it. Scoring the back first allows you to snap the waste piece forward and cut along the face side after the panel is hung and the sides are cut (see the top photos on p. 54).

If you want to do a fast job and you don't mind the dust it generates, use a drywall router to cut the opening. Just attach the panel and follow along the inside of the opening in a counterclockwise direction.

■ **WORK SAFE**
■ **WORK**
■ **THINKING AHEAD**

When using a drywall saw, cut from the face side to avoid damaging the finish paper.

For precise and easier cuts around the tops of windows and doors, score the height of the opening on the back of the panel before attaching it.

Before installing drywall over a window opening, score the back of the panel at window-header height. Here the author has already cut along the sides of the opening and is snapping the pre-scored section forward.

Score the front side with a utility knife to remove the piece.

You can use a drywall router to cut out a window opening. Guide the bit along the inside of the framing around the window opening.

Cutting holes for small openings

Cutting out holes for electrical outlet boxes, switches, and other small openings is trickier than making continuous straight cuts. However, with a little practice and some careful measuring, it's really not that hard to master. There are a few ways to mark and cut the openings, but the main distinction is whether you make the cuts before or after you hang the panel.

To cut an opening before hanging a panel, measure the box's coordinates and transfer them to the panel. However, the problem with this method is that the box never seems to line up perfectly with the cut opening. This misalignment is because the wall, floor, or attached panel isn't perfectly square or level or has gaps. Even if everything is square, it's still pretty easy to make a mistake with this method. Some outlet covers and fixtures barely cover a ¼-in. area around the box, so absolute precision is important or

you'll need to patch later (see p. 146). Another method you can use on walls is to rub the face of the outlet box with chalk and then press the panel against it. The chalk leaves an outline of the box on the back of the panel.

Because of the potential for error with the "cut first" method, I prefer to cut out boxes after the drywall is tacked in place, which is faster and more accurate. Notice that I said "tacked in place." Use only enough fasteners to keep the panel from falling, and don't nail or screw to the stud or joist to which the box is attached. Fastening too close to the box could put pressure on it, causing the drywall to break apart when you make the cut (see p. 71).

Another way to mark a square or rectangular opening is to use a framing square to transfer the location of the sides of the opening to the drywall. Mark the exact location of each side of the opening on the floor and write down the height of the top and bottom of the box

For accurate cuts around electrical outlets and switch boxes, make the cuts with the panel tacked in place.

WORK SAFE
WORK
THINKING AHEAD

1. To cut an opening for an outlet box, use a framing square to mark the sides and height of the box on the floor.

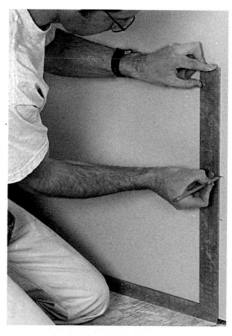

2. Tack the drywall in place, and then transfer the measurements to the face of the panel with the framing square.

3. Cut out the box with a utility saw, being careful to decrease pressure on the panel as you near the end of the cut to avoid blowout.

When using a router, only the center needs to be located. Here a utility saw marks the outlet that was located by sighting over the top of the panel.

Another method for locating the center of a box is to mark the position on the floor, as shown here.

(see photo 1 on p. 55). After tacking the panel in place, transfer the measurements to the drywall using the square (photo 2 on p. 55), and then carefully cut out the opening with a utility saw (photo 3 on p. 55). Bear in mind that the box usually sticks out past the framing the thickness of the drywall, so you need to cut around the *outside* of the box. Round boxes on walls and ceilings can be cut out just as easily, though the method of marking the location is a little different (see the sidebar on the facing page).

An alternative to cutting out electrical boxes with a utility saw is to use an electric drywall router. Before routing an

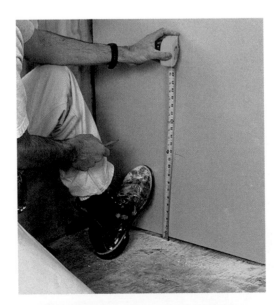

Find the center location of the outlet by transferring measurements to the panel that is tacked in place.

Cut to the edge of the box, and then hop the bit over to the outside edge and router in a counterclockwise direction. Use light pressure as you guide the tip of the cutting bit along the box.

Cutting Round Openings

The most accurate way to cut out an opening for a round fixture box is to measure the box's coordinates, tack the drywall panel in place, transfer the measurements to the panel, and then make the cut.

1. To mark the location of a fixture box, first measure the location of the top and bottom, then the left and right sides. Write down these measurements.

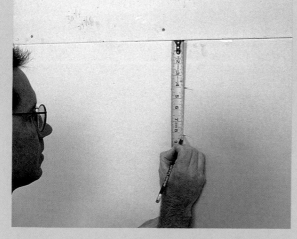

2. Tack the panel in place, and then transfer the measurements to the panel face.

3. Carefully cut around the outside edge of the box with a utility saw.

4. The panel fits snugly around the box.

Carrying Drywall

Carrying a drywall panel is a two-person job. Both carriers should be on the same side of the panel, with the same hand under the bottom edge and the other hand steadying the top. They should hold the panel 1 ft. or more in from each end and let the panel lean against their shoulders. Working together like this is the least strenuous way to carry drywall. However, if you are forced to work alone, there are a number of specialized carrying tools available (see the photos below).

Carrying a drywall panel is usually a two-person job.

A drywall cart works well for carrying single or multiple sheets.

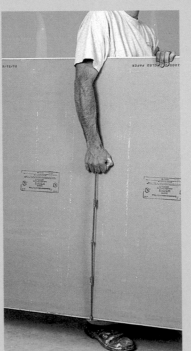

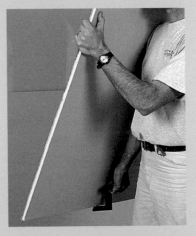

Special tools for carrying drywall make working alone less strenuous. The longer extendable carrier (left) is called The Troll™, by Telpro Inc. The smaller carrier (above) is a Pocket Kart®, by Diversified Tools, Inc.

outlet box, however, first make sure the power is off and the electrical wires are pushed far enough into the box so that the router bit will not reach them. (The router bit should stick out of the router only about ¼ in. more than the thickness of the drywall.) Next, measure from the center of the box to the nearest wall or floor and make a mark. Tack the panel in place and locate the center of the box. With the router running, push the bit through the panel and gently move it until you feel it hit the side of the box. Pull the bit out and hop it over to the outside of the box. Apply light pressure against the box and push the router around it in a counterclockwise direction.

You can also use the router for cutting out larger openings, such as those for heat ducts and vents. The tool takes a little getting used to, but it makes a nice clean cut, and it's fast. The only drawback with using a router is that it generates a lot of fine dust, so wear an approved dust mask.

General Guidelines for Hanging Drywall

A properly planned drywalling job is a team effort, and within the team each person should have specific responsibilities. When drywalling an entire house, my crew and I start by hanging all the large ceilings first. With a crew of three, two people can measure, cut, and lift the panels into position, and the third can screw the panels down and cut out any electrical boxes. Once the ceilings are attached, we usually follow the same procedure for the walls, hanging all the larger panels as a team first and then splitting up to fit and hang all the smaller pieces individually.

It is difficult for one person working alone to hang an 8-ft. piece of drywall on

a ceiling or even on the upper part of a wall. Having enough help is important, especially since it's preferable to hang longer lengths of drywall. Use panels that span the entire length of a wall or ceiling whenever possible.

If one panel doesn't cover the length, still use long panels to avoid having too many butted seams. A butted seam is when the ends—not the tapered edges—of two panels are butted together. There are two potential problems here. One is that both ends are attached to the same 1½-in. framing member. If one panel is cut a little long, there won't be much space to attach the other panel. The result is a toenailed panel that will more than likely be damaged. The other problem is that a butted seam is a weak joint. Any expansion or contraction in the framing or drywall will result in a cracked or ridged seam. So take care when measuring and attaching butted seams, and always stagger butted seams away from each other and away from the center of a wall or ceiling. (See p. 129 for some alternatives for butted seams.)

WORK SAFE
■ **WORK SMART**
■ **THINKING AHEAD**

Before using an electric drywall router to cut a hole for an electrical outlet box, make sure the power is off and the electrical wires are pushed well back into the box.

Fastening Drywall

The preferred method for attaching drywall to wood or metal framing is with drywall screws. Screws are inserted with a drywall screw gun so that the screw head sits just below the surface of the panel without breaking the face paper (see the left photo on p. 60). With the screw gun set to the correct depth, the screw pulls the panel tight against the framing; when the screw stops turning, the clutch disengages. The screw head spins the paper as it sinks in, leaving a slight dimple and a clean smooth edge around it.

Fastener Spacing

Framing Type	Framing Spacing	Maximum Fastener Spacing
Ceiling joists	16 in. o.c., 24 in. o.c.	12 in., 10 in.
Wall studs	16 in. o.c., 24 in. o.c.	16 in.,16 in.

Make sure you hold the screw gun firmly, as shown in the right photo below, and insert the screw straight (a screw that's even slightly tilted will not set deep enough and may tear the face paper). Space the screws evenly on each framing member according to the specifications in the chart above. Place screws at least ⅜ in. in from the perimeter of the panel to avoid damaging the edge.

If you use nails instead of drywall screws, make sure you use ring-shank nails specified for attaching drywall to wood framing. As with screws, set the nails at least ⅜ in. in from the edges and follow the same spacing schedule. When the ends of the panels butt against each other, fasten nails every 8 in. along both sides of the joint.

When using nails instead of screws, all nails "in the field" (across the face of the panel) should be double-nailed. Begin nailing at one edge and work toward the opposite edge. To help keep the drywall tight against the framing, apply hand pressure on the panel next to the nail as you drive it in. Set one nail lightly and then set another nail 1½ in. to 2 in. away. Gently hit each nail until the last blow of the drywall hammer firmly sets each one in shallow, uniform dimples. Do not break the paper, and keep damage to the gypsum core in the dimpled area to a minimum.

If you use nails, I recommend that you do so only along the edges of the panel, and then fill in the rest with dry-

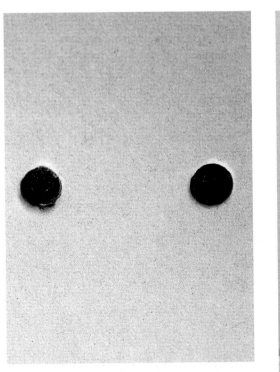

The screw on the left has been installed incorrectly. It is too deep and the head is tearing the face paper around it. The screw on the right is set correctly.

Hold the screw gun firmly as you drive a screw, so that your entire hand and forearm absorb most of the stress.

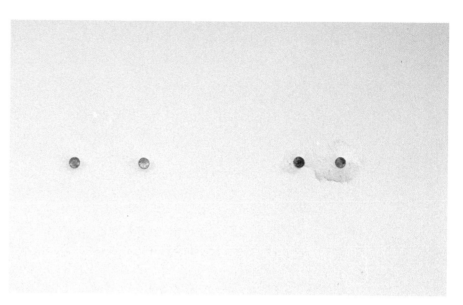

Nails should be set in a shallow dimple (left), not hammered so deep that they break the paper and damage the gypsum core (right).

Space screws approximately 12 in. apart across the face of a ceiling panel. If a screw is set too deep, place another screw next to it and remove any misses.

wall screws in the field. Usually, I tack the panels in place with nails along the edges and then finish the attachment with screws. The object is to get the panel up as quickly as possible, and it's often faster to use nails than screws. Once the panel is tacked in place, I cut out all the openings, and then screw the centers and any spots that I missed along the edges. I prefer to use screws rather than nails along butted seams for a more stable joint.

As discussed in chapter 2, fastener length is important. The problems with using too-short fasteners are obvious, but using too-long fasteners can also present

difficulties. Screws that are too long are likely to tip or go in crooked, damaging the drywall. The longer the nail, the more likely it is to pop as the framing shrinks.

Adhesive technique

Whether you use screws or nails, it takes a lot of fasteners to attach all the panels to a ceiling or wall. One way to cut down on the number of fasteners needed (and to help eliminate the problem of fastener pops and loose panels) is to use the "floating corners" technique, as explained in the sidebar on p. 62. Another fastener-saving method is to secure the drywall with adhesive. I like using adhesives for a number of reasons:

- They reduce the number of fasteners required by up to 75 percent.
- They create a stronger bond than that of nails and screws.
- They are not affected by moisture or by changes in temperature.
- They result in fewer loose panels caused by improper fastening.
- They can bridge minor irregularities in the framing.

▪ **WORK SAFE**
▪ **WORK** SMARTER
▪ **THINKING AHEAD**

When nailing or screwing along the bottom of a panel or along the edge of a doorway or window, place fasteners as close as possible to the panel edge (but no closer than ⅜ in.). The trim will cover these fasteners, which means a few less screws or nails to tape.

Floating Corners Technique

The inside corners where wall meets wall or ceiling meets wall are prone to cracking and fastener pops caused by stress at the intersection. One way to reduce fastener problems is to eliminate fasteners at one or both edges in the corners. I call this the "floating corners" technique.

On ceilings, place the first screw 7 in. to 12 in. in from the edge along the perimeter of the ceiling. When the top panel of the wall is pushed up against the ceiling, it will support the edges of the ceiling panels. Screw in the upper edge of the top wall panel, about 8 in. to 12 in. down from the ceiling.

For the vertical corners on wall panels, omit fasteners on the first panel installed in the corner (see the drawing below). When you fasten the abutting panel, it helps support the first one. Follow this method for the entire height of the

wall corner. Screw or nail the remaining ceiling and wall areas using standard fastening procedures. By eliminating the fasteners in the corners, the drywall is still held firmly in place, but if the corner framing flexes or settles a little, the corners will most likely be unaffected. (Corners that are not fastened still need to have standard wood framing behind them.)

Another version of the floating corner technique uses drywall clips to hold the panels in place. Once attached to the edge of a panel, drywall clips have a nailing foot that is perpendicular to the face of the panel. This allows you to attach both sides of an inside corner to the same stud, eliminating the need for a third stud on an inside corner and backup framing along ceiling edges. When using a drywall clip on a ceiling, keep the first screw back about 18 in. from the edge.

A drywall clip attached to the end of the panel holds the panel in place when a stud is missing along the wall or ceiling edge.

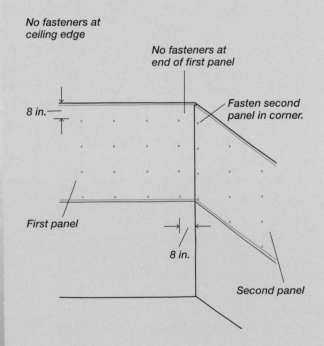

No fasteners at ceiling edge

No fasteners at end of first panel

8 in.

Fasten second panel in corner.

First panel

8 in.

Second panel

Use an adhesive that is approved for wood-to-drywall applications. Apply a ⅜-in.-wide bead to each framing member to within 6 in. of the drywall edges. Wherever the panels butt together, apply a bead of adhesive to each edge of the framing member. Install fasteners along the perimeter of each panel immediately after it is hung.

On panels attached horizontally to walls, no face nailing or screwing is necessary, except on butted seams, and then only enough to form a flush finish (every 10 in. to 12 in.). If panels are attached vertically, the face should be screwed into each stud at 24-in. centers. For ceilings, install one screw every 24 in. (you can remove the screw after 24 hours to cut down on the number of fasteners).

When using adhesive, it's helpful to pre-bow the panels before you hang them. Stack the panels face side up, with the ends supported on 2×4s (see the drawing below), and leave them overnight. When a pre-bowed panel is fastened around the perimeter, the center is forced tight against the adhesive on the framing, thereby eliminating the need for temporary fasteners. Allow the adhesive to dry for at least 48 hours before starting the taping process. (Note that the adhesive method does not work over a plastic vapor barrier or over insulation where the kraft paper overlaps the framing.)

Applying a bead of drywall adhesive along each framing member reduces screw pop and the number of fasteners you need to use.

Hanging Ceilings

In a room that will have drywall attached to the ceiling as well as to the walls, always attach the ceiling panels first. By hanging the ceiling first, the panels can be cut to slip easily into place, and the wall panels will fit against the ceiling to help support the edges.

I usually use adjustable step-up benches to hang ceilings that are 9 ft. high or less. Center the benches under the section to be hung and lift one end of

Pre-Bowing Drywall

Pre-bowing drywall panels prior to adhesive application ensures a tight bond.

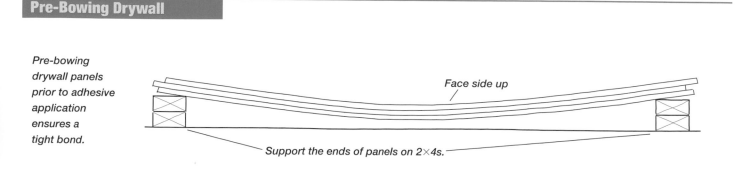

Face side up

Support the ends of panels on 2×4s.

Hang ceilings first. Keep one end of the panel low while you position the other end.

Support the panel with gentle head pressure as you prepare to tack it in place.

the panel into position. Keep the other end low, and then push it into position as a coworker holds the higher end in place (see the top photo at left). Once it is in place, hold the panel against the framing by applying gentle pressure with the top of your head while you fasten it. Alternatively, you can use a T-support to hold the panel in place (see the photo on p. 29).

I know a few drywall hangers who use stilts when attaching drywall. One crew member on the floor does the cutting and hands the panel to two other crew members on stilts. They in turn lift the panel into place on the ceiling and attach it, cut openings for any electrical boxes, and take the next measurement. Under ideal conditions, working on stilts is the fastest way to hang drywall on ceilings, but I prefer not to use them for this job. The two members on stilts can't cut and carry panels, which means a lot of work for the person on the floor. In addition, the work area must be kept clean and uncluttered to minimize the risk of falls.

My favorite way to hang high ceilings, especially cathedral ceilings up to 15 ft. high, is to use a panel lift (see the photo on the facing page). This tool does the heavy lifting while I position the panel. And once I've aligned the panel, the lift holds it in place while I attach it.

Ceiling panels can be hung perpendicular to the joists or parallel to the joists. I prefer to attach the ceiling panels perpendicular to the joists for a number of reasons:

- Ceiling panels are less likely to sag when hung in this direction (see the sidebar on p. 66).
- It allows the butted seams to be attached to a solid nailer for the length of the seam or floated between the joists, as described on p. 129.

When using a lift to install a cathedral ceiling, hang from the top down. If you are lifting the panels yourself, start at the bottom of the ceiling and work up.

- It is easier to see the joists when fastening the panels.
- It gives the structure greater strength.
- It won't matter that much (and may not even be noticed) if the o.c. spacing of a ceiling joist is off.
- It allows the drywall to float over slightly uneven joists, making them less conspicuous.

The only time I hang drywall parallel to the joists is when it will avoid creating butted seams on the ceiling or when the method of application affects the fire rating or structural design. Before opting for this method, though, check the spacing of the joists carefully—they must be spaced so that the edge of each panel falls on the center of a joist. If the tapered edges don't hit on center, you may have to cut the long edge of the panel, which will create a long butted seam. Also, be careful not to create a seam on a joist that is either crowned up or sagged down, as it will be difficult to hide when taping.

No matter the direction in which the panels are hung, if you cannot avoid butted seams, stagger them and keep them as far away as possible from the center of the ceiling. Discontinuous butted seams are easier to conceal and less likely to crack. (For more on butted seams, see chapter 6.)

Before hanging drywall, some ceilings are first furred with 1×3s perpendicular to

WORK SAFE
WORK SMART
THINKING AHEAD

When hanging a cathedral ceiling, it's easier to attach the lower panel first, and then work your way up to the top. By starting at the bottom, you'll have an edge for the next panel to rest on while you hang it. This is easier than trying to lift a panel up to fit against the bottom edge of the panel above it.

Grain Orientation in Drywall

In chapter 1, I listed the maximum o. c. framing spacing for the various types and thicknesses of drywall. In many instances, however, the framing must be closer if the ceiling panels are hung parallel to the joists. I've known this to be true since I started drywalling, but I never really gave too much thought as to why. After reading an article about grain orientation in drywall in *Fine Homebuilding* magazine (#98), I now understand the reason.

Arden Van Norman performed a simple test to prove that drywall is stronger with the grain than across it. He cut one 1-ft. by 4-ft. piece from the end of a panel and one from the side, as shown in the drawing below. Stacking bricks in the middle of each piece quickly shows that the end piece is much weaker than the side one. Drywall is approximately three times stronger in the long direction. Accordingly, drywall hung perpendicular to the framing members is stronger than drywall hung parallel, so it is less likely to sag.

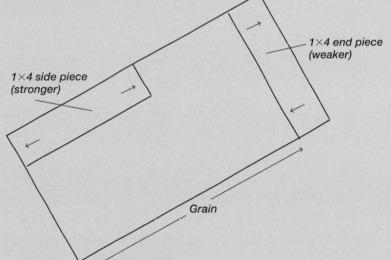

1×4 side piece (stronger)

1×4 end piece (weaker)

Grain

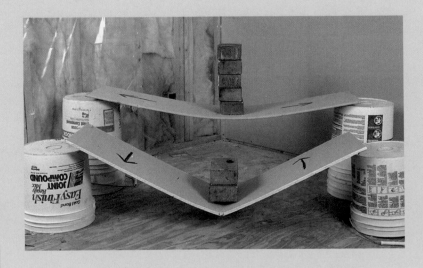

A simple test proves that drywall is stronger with the grain than across it.

the joists. A ceiling may be furred for a number of reasons: to help straighten out a wavy ceiling, to decrease the distance between the nailers (ceiling joists), or to provide solid nailing over rigid insulation. The 2½-in.-wide strips make an excellent target when fastening the drywall. The strips should be treated just like ceiling joists, and the drywall should be hung following the same procedures.

Hanging Walls

Once you've attached all the ceilings, it's time to start working on the walls. It is usually a lot easier to hang walls than ceilings. You may have to make more cuts for electrical boxes and other openings, but at least you're not working over your head. Before hanging walls, it's a good idea to mark the location of the wall studs on the ceiling and floor to make them easier to locate once they are covered. Also, mark the location of electrical boxes and other openings that will be cut out after the drywall is attached (see p. 55).

As with ceilings, you can hang wall panels in one of two ways—horizontally or vertically. In commercial work, walls are often higher than 8 ft., so it makes sense to hang drywall vertically to reduce seams. On walls that are longer than 16 ft., hanging drywall vertically helps eliminate butted seams. However, for walls that are 8 ft. high or less (or 9 ft. high if I'm using 54-in. panels), I usually prefer to hang drywall horizontally. Here's why:

- It decreases the linear footage of seams that need taping by up to 25 percent (see the drawing on p. 14).
- It provides extra bracing strength, because more studs are tied together.
- It makes the seams easier to hide, because light usually shines along finished seams, which makes them less obvious. When the seams are perpendicular to the studs, they simply flow over any studs that may not be perfectly straight, helping hide imperfections.

Start nails along the top edge of the top panel before lifting the sheet into place.

Attaching Drywall to Metal Framing

Drywall can be hung on metal framing in much the same way as it is on wood framing, but there are a couple of things to note. Metal studs and joists are made out of a thin piece of steel bent into a C-shaped stud. Before attaching drywall to the metal studs, check to see which direction the open side of the stud faces (they should all be installed in the same direction). On a long wall that will have butted seams or when hung vertically, the drywall should be attached from the end that the open side of the stud faces (see the drawing below).

For the seams to end up flat, the drywall must be attached in the proper sequence. Fasten the edge of the first panel to the unsupported open edge of the stud. Screw on the entire length of the panel before attaching the abutting panel. If the panel were first attached to the solid side and then to the unsupported side, the screw may deflect the open end and force the panel edges outward. When screwing on the rest of the panel, keep the screws closer to the solid edge of the stud. (Note that you should always use screws, not nails, when fastening drywall to metal framing.)

Top view

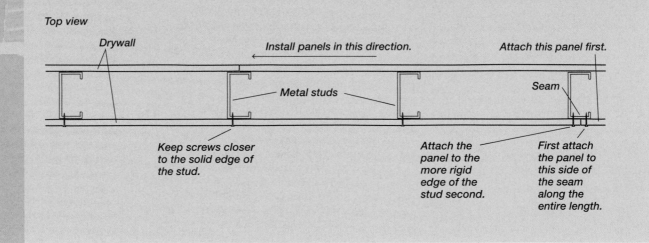

Drywall

Install panels in this direction.

Attach this panel first.

Metal studs

Seam

Keep screws closer to the solid edge of the stud.

Attach the panel to the more rigid edge of the stud second.

First attach the panel to this side of the seam along the entire length.

■ It makes the seams easier to tape, because they are at a convenient working height.

To hang drywall horizontally, hang the top panel first, fitting it tightly against the ceiling. If the wall has a window, cut the panel to length first. Then use a utility knife to score the back at the top of the window opening (see p. 54). Now stand the panel on the floor exactly below where it will be attached, leaning it against the studs. Start a nail about 1 in. down, lining it up with each stud. Lift the panel up against the ceiling and drive the nails home.

After the top of the panel is nailed in place, cut out any small openings. Then fasten the rest of the panel and cut out any window or door openings. Next, cut the bottom panel to fit against the top panel. This panel should be about ½ in. shorter in height, so that it will not fit tightly against the floor and break apart when it is fastened into place. Cutting it a little short also leaves room for you to slide a panel lifter or a prybar underneath, so that you can lift the drywall into place (see the drawing on p. 70). Most electrical outlets are located near the floor, so tack just the top of the panel, and then cut out the electrical

Lift the panel up against the ceiling and nail it in place.

As long as the extension jambs are not in place, a window opening can be cut out with a saw. If the jambs are in place, use a router or cut out the opening before hanging the drywall.

Using a Panel Lifter

Slide the lift under the bottom edge of the panel.

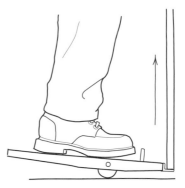

Bear down on the back end of the lift to raise the panel.

A panel lifter slides under a sheet of drywall and, as its name suggests, lifts the panel into place, so that you can focus on attaching it.

boxes as explained on p. 55. Remember not to put too much pressure on the panel, which could cause the face to break apart around the box (see the top photo on the facing page).

As with ceilings, butted seams should be staggered and placed away from the center of a wall. Butted seams can also be located above doors and above or below windows to create a shorter seam. Try to keep the seam at least 8 in. in from the edge of an opening, because the wall is more stable there. Also, the slight crown that forms during taping could affect the trim miter joint if the seam is located at the corner.

When hanging panels on an outside corner, run the panels long and trim them after they're attached (you can use the same technique on a bottom panel that adjoins a door opening). Running the panel long means taking one less measurement, and it also allows some flexibility if the inside corners are not plumb and need to be scribed to fit. If the framing isn't square or plumb at the outside corner, the panel can be cut to fit the exact angle, so that there won't be any big gaps under the corner bead.

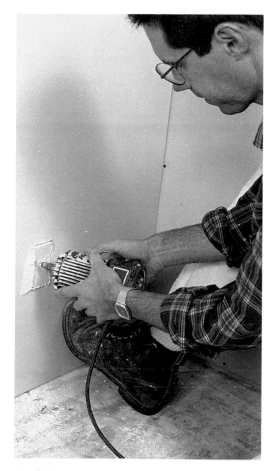

Applying too much pressure with your foot as you cut an opening for an electrical box can break the face of the panel.

Summary for Hanging Drywall

- Always hang ceilings first.
- Don't cut panels so that they fit too tightly, and never force panels into place.
- Place tapered edges together whenever possible.
- Try to hang panels perpendicular to the framing.
- Try to span the length of a wall or ceiling with one panel.
- Stagger butted seams away from each other and away from the center of a wall or ceiling.
- When hanging a cathedral ceiling, start at the bottom edge of the ceiling.
- Cut out electrical boxes and other small openings after the panels are tacked in place.
- Use screws rather than nails (and only screws with metal framing).
- Use screws and adhesive for best results.
- Fasten drywall close to the edges of doorways and windows and along the floor to avoid having to tape those fasteners.
- Attach corner bead to all outside corners, uncased openings, beams, and soffits.

Run panels long at doorways and outside corners, and then cut off the excess after the panels are attached.

Hanging a Garage

Garages, which are typically large rooms with high ceilings, require a somewhat different hanging strategy than most rooms within a house. Garage ceilings are usually too large to cover without butted seams, so I almost always hang the drywall perpendicular to the joists. If the ceiling is over 9 ft. high, I often hang the garage walls parallel to the studs—that is, vertically rather than horizontally. By standing the panels on end, I avoid having any butted seams on the walls. If you hang wall panels vertically, just make sure that the studs are reasonably straight and that the seams will fall on the studs.

Gable walls

For gable ends of a room with a cathedral or sloped ceiling, I usually hang the bottom panel first (see the drawing below). The floor is a good flat surface from which to measure, and the bottom panel usually has a square end for at least part of the height. The second panel can be measured from the bottom panel. Setting the panels on top of each other makes it easier to hold them in place, especially when the ceiling is high. Note that you should not locate or fasten a butted seam on the center support of the gable end. The building may move or settle at that point, causing stress to the drywall.

Hanging a Gable Wall

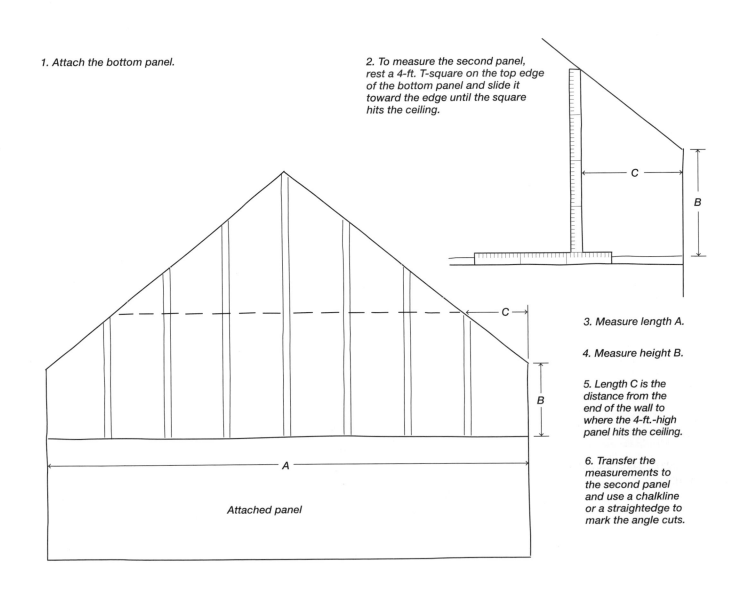

1. Attach the bottom panel.

2. To measure the second panel, rest a 4-ft. T-square on the top edge of the bottom panel and slide it toward the edge until the square hits the ceiling.

C

B

C

Attached panel

B

A

3. Measure length A.

4. Measure height B.

5. Length C is the distance from the end of the wall to where the 4-ft.-high panel hits the ceiling.

6. Transfer the measurements to the second panel and use a chalkline or a straightedge to mark the angle cuts.

Work from the bottom up when attaching drywall to a gable end wall.

Use a T-square to lay out measurements for an angle cut.

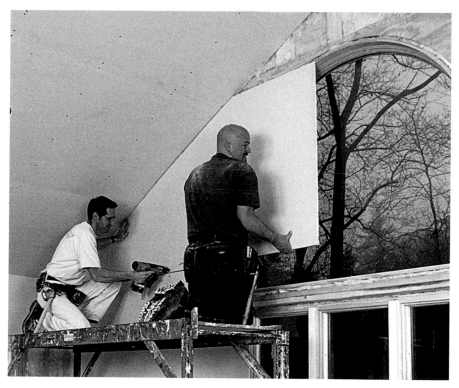

Setting the second panel on top of the first helps to hold it in place while fastening.

WORK SAFE
WORK ▪▪▪▪▪▪
THINKING AHEAD

Make sure the edges of corner bead lie flat against the wall (they shouldn't stick out past the raised bead on the outside corner edge). Use more fasteners if the edges don't hug the wall tightly.

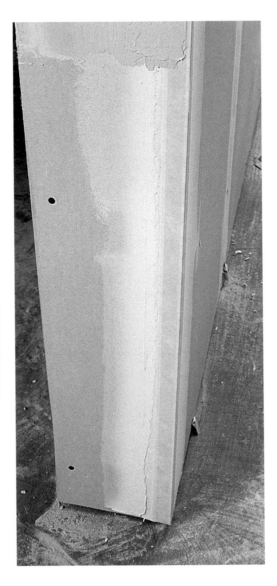

For wall installations, keep the bead off the floor about ½ in. to avoid potential problems should the building move or settle.

Corner bead resists impact and provides a straight edge for taping.

Trim Accessories

After the drywall has been attached, you should protect all outside corners, uncased openings, beams, and soffits with corner bead. Corner bead resists impact and forms a straight raised edge for taping. Whenever possible, it should be installed in one piece. Cut the bead with trim snips approximately ½ in. short and push it tight against the ceiling. Leaving the corner bead a little short reduces the risk of the bead binding and coming loose or cracking should the wall settle. The baseboard will cover the gap along the floor. If more than one piece is required, butt beads together—don't overlap them. Make sure that the butted ends are even with each other and that they lie straight.

As mentioned in chapter 2, there are a number of corner and trim beads available. Below is a brief explanation of how they are attached.

Metal beads

When attached to drywall hung over wood framing, galvanized metal bead is usually nailed in place. When attaching it to drywall hung over metal framing, use a corner crimper, $\frac{9}{16}$-in. staples, or screws that go through the drywall and into the framing. If you use a crimper, crimp the corner every 4 in. to 6 in. When using screws, nails, or staples, attach the bead every 9 in., placing pairs of fasteners opposite each other on either side of the corner.

There is also a metal bead with barbed edges that hold the bead in place, requiring a minimal number of fasteners. Use hand pressure or a rubber mallet to push the bead into place. A fastener at each end or at the center may be necessary to help align this type of bead.

Vinyl beads

There are a lot of vinyl beads on the market, and all of them can be installed in any one of three ways. First, dry-fit the bead for length and check it for proper fit. From there, you have three options. The first is to attach both legs of the bead every 6 in. to 10 in. with ½-in.-long staples. The second is to spray vinyl adhesive on the drywall and then on the bead, and then immediately attach the bead to the corner, pressing the legs into place (see the photos on p. 76). You can also use staples with adhesive to create an even stronger corner. The third option is to set the bead in joint compound, and then press the bead into place until the compound exudes through the holes and the bead is straight. Then press the legs into place using a taping knife.

Paper-faced beads

Both the paper-faced metal and the plastic beads that I have used are installed with joint compound. You can use either a taping knife or a corner roller to set the bead in the compound. Each brand and type (square or bullnose) has its own specially designed roller tool. Whichever method you use, press the bead into place and embed the paper flanges flat against the wall (see the photos on p. 77).

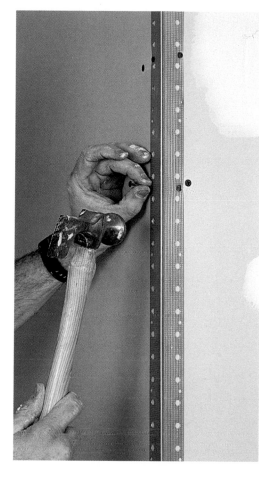

Attach corner bead before taping. When installing metal bead, place nails on both sides of the bead and space the pairs about 8 in. apart.

A corner crimper provides an alternative to nailing. Crimp the bead every 4 in. to 6 in.

WORK SAFE
WORK SMART
THINKING AHEAD

If you're working with the larger bullnose beads, cut the drywall short to accommodate the curve of the bead.

Vinyl bead is more durable than metal bead, especially if it is fastened with adhesive and then stapled.

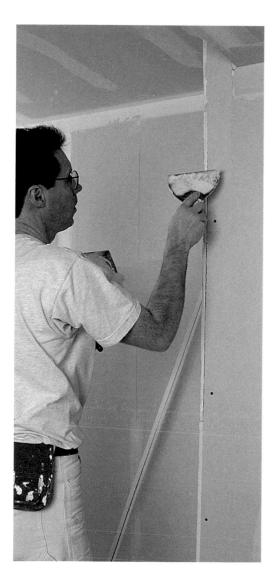

Paper-faced metal and plastic beads are quite durable. To install, apply compound to the wall, align the bead, and then use a roller tool to embed it properly. Remove excess compound with a taping knife.

■ WORK SAFE
■ WORK SMART
■ THINKING AHEAD

Since edge seams often intersect corner beads, install paper-faced beads after the seams have been taped and coated with the first layer of joint compound. The compound fills the tape between panels and provides a more level surface for the corner bead.

CHAPTER 4

Taping

FOR ME, taping over freshly hung drywall is the most enjoyable part of a drywalling job. It's fast-paced work that's not too physically demanding, and it's pretty much dust-free, which is a nice break after the hanging stage. Taping is also the part of the drywalling process that requires the most skill and the most patience. As you'll see, there's more to taping than just concealing the joints between panels. A properly taped joint should be as strong and as durable as the drywall panel itself.

When this book was originally published in 1996, I said that I preferred hand taping to using mechanical taping tools. Times change and so have the tools and my opinions on using them. Now I'm really hooked on mechanical taping tools because they speed up the work and produce a quality application with a consistency that hand taping cannot match.

The taping sequence is the same for both hand taping and taping with mechanical tools. In this chapter, I'll take you step by step through the hand taping sequence followed by a brief description of the mechanical tools, with pros and cons of each method. In addition, I'll describe some common taping problems and ways to avoid and correct them.

We're finally ready to tape, my favorite part of the job.

Taping Basics

Drywall is typically finished, or "taped," with three coats of joint compound, and then lightly sanded to produce a smooth surface suitable for decorating with most types of paints, textures, and wall coverings. Three coats of joint compound are necessary to conceal the joints, corners,

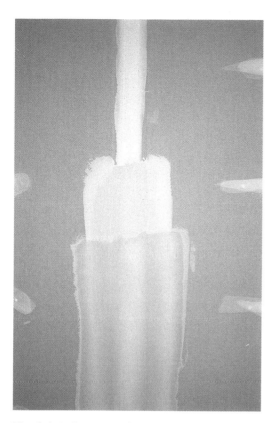

The joints between drywall panels are covered with paper or fiberglass-mesh tape and coated with three layers of joint compound.

and fasteners. In some cases (when applying a setting-type compound, for example), you can get acceptable results with just two coats, but three coats helps ensure a more professional-looking job.

The first coat, which is commonly called the tape-embedding coat or the rough coat, does not have to be perfect. It just has to be neat and of consistent width and thickness. The second coat is the filler coat; this is the time when you hide the joint tape and feather the edges of the joint compound. The third coat, often referred to as the finish coat, is a thin layer of compound applied lightly over the second coat to smooth out any remaining rough areas. Each coat is applied a little wider than the previous coat, and the edges are feathered to leave a smooth surface. Sometimes a thin skim coat is applied to the entire surface after

the third coat is dry. This results in the highest quality finish.

What should be taped

Joint compound alone has little strength, and if a joint between panels were just filled with compound, the joint would inevitably crack. To strengthen the joint, paper or fiberglass-mesh tape must be used with the compound. The compound acts like an adhesive, but it's the tape that actually joins the two panels together. With the tape centered on the joint and embedded in the joint compound, the face paper of the two panels essentially becomes one solid surface. The layers of the joint compound that cover the tape are used to conceal the joint.

The same principle applies to cracks, holes, and hammer marks that tear the surface of the drywall: They all need to be covered with paper or mesh tape to strengthen the surface. Inside corners on walls and ceilings are also joints that

All fasteners, joints between panels, and inside and outside corners require taping.

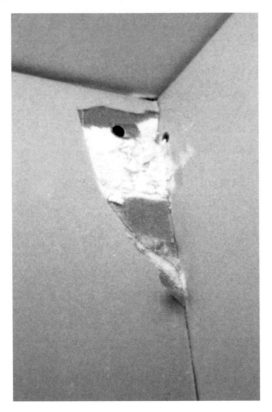

Damaged areas at inside corners (and anywhere else) should be filled with compound before you apply the first coat.

affected by many different circumstances, including the height of the ceiling, the number of joints and corners, the quality of the hanging job, and the temperature and humidity at the job site. I usually plan to take the same amount of time for each coat: If it takes 8 hours to apply the first coat, it will take about 8 hours for the second coat and another 8 hours for the third.

Taping can be a messy job, and it is very difficult to avoid getting joint compound on your hands, your clothes, and the floor. I keep an old taping knife and an empty pail handy so I can scoop up dropped joint compound before it gets walked on. The work area should be clean and uncluttered, so that the walls and ceilings can be finished along their entire length without worrying about tripping or falling (this is especially important if you're working on stilts). Having to move tools, drywall scraps, or building materials from place to place every time you tape can waste a lot of time and lead to frustration and loss of concentration.

need to be strengthened as well as concealed. Paper tape is embedded in the corner and, after it dries, covered with two or more coats of joint compound. Fasteners, dents, and slight imperfections can be concealed with joint compound alone. Since the surface is unbroken, the area is still strong, so tape is unnecessary.

What to expect when taping

Taping requires patience as well as skill. If I apply the first coat of tape and compound on Monday, I wait until Tuesday, when the first coat is fully dry, to go over everything again with the second coat. On Wednesday, I apply the third coat. As each coat of joint compound is applied, I must become more particular, smoothing out the compound to blend in with the surface of the drywall.

The time it takes to finish taping a certain square footage of drywall is

Before you begin

Before you start taping, make sure that all the drywall panels are firmly attached, that all the electrical outlet boxes and other openings have been cut out, and that the corner bead has been installed where necessary. The temperature of the air, joint compound, and drywall surface should be consistent—at least 55°F if you're using drying types of joint compound and 45°F if using setting types. Ideally, the temperature should be 65°F to 70°F. Good ventilation and low humidity also help the joint compound dry and set up properly.

If there are any damaged areas of drywall, such as busted-out inside corners or outlet-box openings, cut away the loose drywall and fill the holes with a coat of joint compound. Also fill any

A taping or setting-type compound is ideal for prefilling gaps before taping.

gaps between panels that are more than ⅛ in. wide. Allow these areas to dry before applying the first coat. If time is of the essence, use setting-type compound as filler (see p. 44).

Mixing joint compound

As explained in chapter 2, joint compounds are available in powdered and ready-mixed forms. I mix powdered compounds (either setting types or drying types) with water in a 5-gal. joint-compound pail, using a heavy-duty ½-in. electric drill with a mixing paddle (see the photos below).

SETTING-TYPE COMPOUND. If you're mixing a setting-type compound, it's especially important to make sure that the pail and mixing paddle are clean, since even a thin film of dry compound on either one can cause the compound to set up prematurely. The hardened compound can also come loose and get mixed in, leaving chunks in the fresh compound.

Follow the directions on the label concerning the proportions of water and compound. Pour the specified amount of cool (not cold or hot), clean water into the pail, and then add the compound. Mix until the compound reaches the

Use a mixing paddle attached to a heavy-duty drill to mix powdered compounds with water.

■ **WORK SAFE**
■ **WORK SMART**
■ **THINKING AHEAD**

If possible, go through the work area the day before you begin taping to fill any gaps larger than ⅛ in. with joint compound. You must fill the gaps anyway, and this way the compound will set up or dry before you begin taping.

Mix the compound until it is stiff enough to hold onto the trowel without sliding off.

desired consistency. It should be stiff enough to hold its form on the trowel (see the photo above), but not so stiff that it is difficult to smooth. Be careful not to overmix, because too much mixing can shorten the hardening time. It's also important not to mix more compound than you can use within the specified time. Once that time has expired, the compound hardens chemically. Don't try to remix any setting-type compound that has started to set up—it's unusable.

DRYING-TYPE COMPOUND. To mix powdered drying-type compound, add the compound to the specified amount of water and mix well until the powder is completely damp. Remix after 15 minutes. This type of compound does not set up—it has to air dry—so it can be kept for

extended periods of time as long as it's covered. It can be remixed, if necessary.

READY-MIXED COMPOUND. If a ready-mixed compound is fresh, just a little stirring is necessary. If it has been sitting around for a while, you'll sometimes need to loosen it by adding a little water. Even if you don't need to add water, it's a good idea to mix the compound so it has the same consistency throughout the pail. I prefer to use a masher-type mixer rather than a powered mixing paddle for ready-mixed compounds; the electric mixer can whip air into the compound, which can cause pitting or bubbles in the taped seams (see p. 104).

Ready-mixed compounds are generally used at the consistency in which they come, but they can be thinned for taping. I often thin the compound for the third coat. Add a little water at a time to avoid overthinning (if the mixture becomes too thin, add more compound

When loosening ready-mixed joint compound, use a masher-type mixer to avoid adding too much air to the compound.

to attain the correct consistency). If the compound freezes, allow it to thaw at room temperature and mix it without adding water. If the compound has sat too long and separated so that a clear liquid forms on top, it can usually be remixed. If it smells sour or looks moldy, the compound has gone bad and should not be used.

An efficient taping system

When I start a room, I apply a coat of joint compound to all fasteners in the field on a wall, then embed tape on the seams, and then embed tape in the corners. If there is an outside corner, I finish the section by applying a coat of joint compound over the corner bead before progressing to the next wall. This is an efficient way of taping rather than first taping all fasteners, then walking around the job again and taping only seams, and so on. In the interest of clarity, however, I'll present all the information on taping fasteners, taping seams, taping inside corners, and taping outside corners in separate sections.

Taping Sequence

If you're just learning to tape, it's probably easiest to go from room to room and apply the first coat to all the fastener heads. Then go back and do all the flat seams between panels. When those are dry, apply the first coat to the inside and outside corners. Working this way means that you won't worry about messing up a flat seam when you're working on a corner, which can be a problem when the seam is still wet.

Once you have the hang of taping, work in this sequence to speed the job along:

1. Fasteners
2. Tapered-edge seams
3. Butted seams
4. Inside corners
5. Outside corners

To save time as you're taping, make sure you have all the taping tools you may need handy—in your hands, in your back pocket, or near a pail of joint compound. And keep the pail of joint compound close by, moving it with you as you tape.

tapering the edges brings the indentations level with the panel surface and requires only minimal sanding. Apply the second and third coats at the same time you second- and third-coat the seams in the room.

Taping Fastener Heads

I like to tape fastener (screw and nail) heads first, so that I don't accidentally mess up a seam that I've already taped. You need only a thin layer of joint compound to conceal the fasteners, and it's easiest to tape a row of two or three fasteners in a single strip rather than individually (see the photo at right). Using a 5-in. or 6-in. taping knife, apply just enough pressure to fill the indentation and leave the face of the drywall panel covered with a very thin film of compound. Don't be tempted to fill the indentation with one thick coat; applying three thin coats of compound and

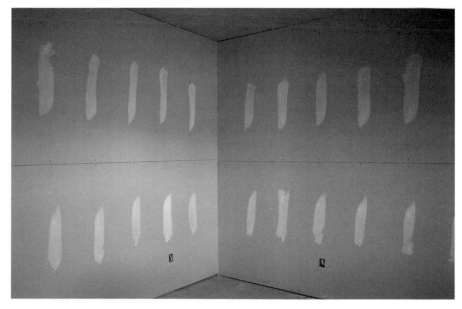

Fasteners are easier to conceal when they are taped in strips of two or three rather than individually.

Taping Seams

There are two types of drywall seams: tapered-edge seams between panels and butted seams, which are created when nontapered panel ends are joined together. Remember that you should try to keep butted seams to a minimum (see chapter 1).

First coat

The seams between drywall panel edges take considerably longer to first-coat than do fastener heads, because they require an application of tape as well as joint compound. There are two ways to tape these seams: with fiberglass-mesh tape or with paper tape.

MESH-TAPE METHOD. I usually use self-adhesive fiberglass-mesh tape rather than paper tape on the tapered-edge seams between panels (see p. 42). Mesh tape is

Use an all-purpose or taping compound, not a topping compound, for the first coat on seams. Although a topping compound is fine for finish coats, it is not suitable for the first coat because of potential problems with adhering to the fastener heads.

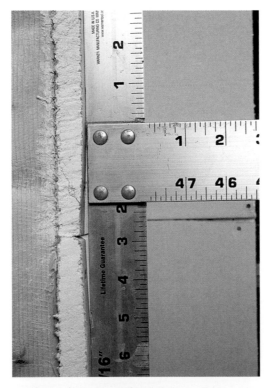

The taper along the long edge of a drywall panel creates a recessed joint when you butt two panels together.

fast and easy to use, and you don't have to worry about loose tape and air bubbles under the tape, which can be problems with paper tape.

On the downside, mesh tape is not as strong as paper tape, so it's important to use the right type of joint compound with it. You can embed mesh tape in any type of setting-type compound, but if you're working with drying-type compounds, make sure you use a taping compound, not a topping or an all-purpose compound (see p. 43). I prefer to use a setting-type compound, which is stronger and shrinks and cracks very little when drying.

When using mesh tape, apply the tape to all the joints in the room before applying the joint compound. Press the tape firmly over the joint so it lies flat with no wrinkles, and cut it to length with a sharp taping knife or a utility knife. Using a hawk or a large (4 in. by 14 in.) beveled trowel as a palette, apply joint compound to the entire length of the joint with a 5-in. or 6-in. taping knife. Put a small amount of compound on the taping knife and press the compound onto the center of the joint for the width of the trowel. A thin, even layer of ¼-in.-thick compound is all that you need. Don't worry about the compound being too smooth at this point.

Now switch to the 4 in. by 14 in. beveled trowel to smooth the compound. With the trowel centered on the seam and held almost flat against the panels, pull the trowel along the joint, smoothing the compound with the back edge. Leave a layer of compound that just covers the tape and fills the recessed areas of the tapered seam. The edges should be fairly smooth and feathered. If a lot of compound builds up in front of the trowel and pushes out around the sides as you smooth the seam, either you have put too much joint compound on the

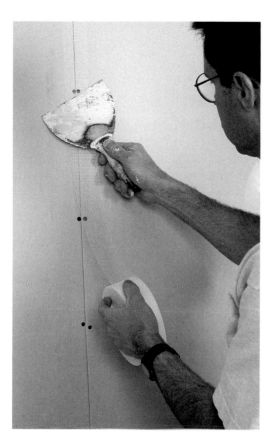

Self-adhesive mesh tape strengthens the joint between the tapered edges of two drywall panels.

To cover the mesh tape, apply a thin layer of compound the width of the knife and smooth it with a knife or curved trowel.

seam or you're taking too much off. When you've finished the seam, the joint compound should be about ³⁄₁₆ in. thick in the center and 6 in. or less wide from one tapered edge to the other. Remember: The first coat doesn't have to be perfect—just make sure that you don't build up the compound too thickly and don't leave ridges that will make the application of the second coat more difficult.

PAPER-TAPE METHOD. While mesh tape works fine on the tapered-edge seams between panels, it isn't as strong as paper tape, so I avoid using it on butted seams. Those seams need the extra strength of paper tape to reduce the risk of cracking (which is greater for butted seams, because they are typically spliced on a single stud or joist). Unlike mesh tape, paper tape forms a strong joint on seams when it is used with any type of tape-embedding joint compound. Paper tape used in conjunction with an all-purpose joint compound is the most common way to tape seams (whether they are tapered edge or butted).

The procedure for embedding paper tape is somewhat different than for that of mesh tape. Because the paper tape is not self-adhesive, you first have to lay down a ground coat of compound to hold the paper in place. Use a 5-in. or 6-in. taping knife to apply a thin, fairly even layer of joint compound ¼ in. thick or less along the center of the seam. (Note that you can work on more than one seam at a time but usually not on every seam in the room. The compound may start to dry before you are able to do the last seams, making it more difficult to

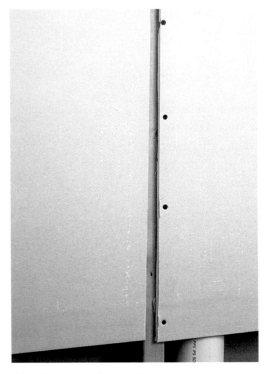

A butted seam is created when the non-tapered ends of two panels are joined together. Here the second piece is being slid into place.

Butted seams are prone to cracking, so it's preferable to use paper tape to strengthen the joint. Apply a layer of compound, and then center the tape along the entire length of the seam.

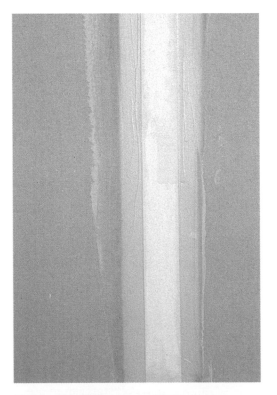

Firmly embed the tape with the taping knife, squeezing out excess compound and feathering the edges as you go.

■ **WORK SAFE**
■ **WORK**
■ **THINKING AHEAD**

Keep wrinkles out of paper tape by leaving a smooth, even layer of compound under the tape.

work with and more likely to form air bubbles behind the paper tape.) Next, center the paper tape on the joint and press it very lightly into place. Keep the tape pulled tight and reasonably straight along the joint. Rip the tape to the desired length, making sure that the tape goes far enough into each corner so that the corner tape overlaps the joint tape.

With the paper tape in position, pull the taping knife along the center of the tape. I usually start at the center of a seam and pull toward each end. (If the joint butts into an inside corner, be careful not to leave too much compound under the tape as you approach the corner to avoid raising a bump.) Keep enough pressure on the knife to properly embed the tape as you go. The pressure on the knife should push the extra compound out from the edges, leaving a layer ⅛ in. thick or less under the tape. Make sure the tape is flat, wrinkle-free, and setting-type compound can be used for the second coat. Before you begin, check the surface and knock off any noticeable ridges or chunks of hardened compound with the edge of the taping knife. Smooth areas and blend them together as necessary, but keep in mind that there's still one more coat of compound to apply, so everything doesn't have to be perfect.

TAPERED-EDGE SEAMS. The second coat of joint compound is usually applied to seams after the inside corners are second-coated (see p. 91). Using a 6-in. taping knife and a 4-in. by 14-in. beveled trowel, apply the compound about 8 in. wide, with the seam in the center. The coat should be about 3/16 in. thick and fairly even. Whenever possible, apply the compound to the entire length of the seam before you start smoothing it with

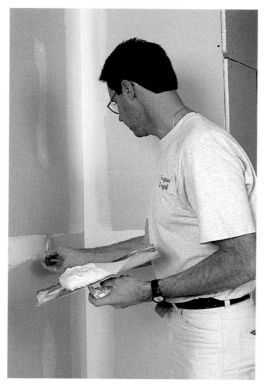

Use a 6-in. taping knife to apply the second coat of compound over seams. Apply the compound approximately 8 in. wide.

tight against the panel at the edges. Clean excess compound from along the edges of the joint with the taping knife. As when using mesh tape, make sure the first coat is no more than 6 in. wide.

Try to tape the entire joint with one length of tape. If the paper tape wrinkles or bunches up as you embed it with the taping knife, it's probably because you applied the initial layer of compound too thickly or you didn't pull the tape tightly enough when you put it in place. If you must use two pieces of tape, say, on a joint over 20 ft. long, work from the corner toward the center, where the two pieces overlap.

Second coat

The second coat of joint compound, also known as the filler coat, is the step when the largest amount of joint compound is applied and the seams are filled and widened. An all-purpose, topping or

■ WORK SAFE
■ WORK
■ THINKING AHEAD

Keep butted seams above a door or window away from the edge of the opening. This makes the joint stronger and eliminates having a slight bump where the mitered edges of the trim will be.

Position butted seams above or below an opening a few inches in from the edge. Embed paper tape in a layer of joint compound, and then smooth out the joint with a taping knife.

Taping at Ceiling Level

For best results, I prefer to tape the entire length of a seam or inside corner in one pass. That's no problem when you're working on a horizontal wall seam 4 ft. from the floor, but ceilings and the tops of inside or outside corners present more of a challenge.

For ceilings 9 ft. high or less, I find that a pair of adjustable stilts allows me the greatest maneuverability for taping joints and fasteners. If stilts are not practical for you (or if you're not allowed to use them for drywalling where you live), set up a plank long enough to work the length of a seam at an appropriate height. For ceilings over 9 ft. high, you'll have to set up some kind of scaffolding, as discussed on p. 31.

In most rooms, all you need to reach the top of an inside or outside corner is an overturned, empty joint-compound pail. I find it easiest to work from the top down.

Working on stilts allows you to tape seams and corners in one pass without using staging.

Setting a plank on two joint-compound pails below a seam provides a simple way to reach the ceiling.

The top of most inside corners can be reached by standing on an empty joint-compound pail.

the beveled trowel. Keep the trowel almost flat and apply pressure to the outside edges of the seam, feathering the edges as you pull the trowel along. Some compound will be removed as the edges are feathered.

Next, center the trowel and glide it along the joint, applying constant, even pressure to both edges of the seam. Hold the trowel almost flat against the seam with the back edge doing the work. If all goes well, the edges of the seam will remain feathered and the center will be smoothed to an inconspicuous crown. Repeat this method until most of the air bubbles in the joint compound have been removed. The second-coated seam should be about 10 in. wide, and the tape should not be visible. Try not to remove too much joint compound. If you find that you're pulling off too much, you're probably holding the trowel at too steep of an angle. Apply more compound to the seam and try again, this time holding the trowel flatter to the surface.

BUTTED-END SEAMS. Because the butted ends of drywall panels are not recessed, as tapered edges are, you create a slight bump at the joint when you apply the tape and the first coat of compound. To conceal the bump, you need to apply a wider band of compound than you do with tapered-edge seams (you may also need to apply four coats of compound to blend the bump into the drywall surface).

Before applying the second coat to butted seams, I usually run my hand across the joint or hold a straightedge to it to determine how wide I need to spread the joint compound to blend in the seam. The center is the high area, so you need to cover the tape lightly and build up the joint compound along the sides of the tape. Feather the edges, and then smooth the center. Don't apply too much

compound at one time. I usually widen it with a beveled trowel or a 12-in. taping knife to about 10 in. on each side of the tape.

Third coat

If you have been careful with the first and second coats, the third coat should be the easiest and require the least amount of joint compound. Because this is usually the final coat, it is a good idea to do some light sanding before you begin.

Sand all the joints using a pole sander with 100-grit or 120-grit

Use a curved trowel to smooth the compound, keeping the tape concealed and the edges feathered. The finished second coat should be about 10 in. wide.

Checking for Crowned Seams

Once the second coat is dry, check for potential problem seams with a straightedge or the edge of a long trowel. Hold the straightedge on the center of the seam and check the gap on each side. If it's greater than ¹⁄₁₆ in., feather the compound farther out on both sides to conceal the seam. Starting at the center, apply joint compound the width of two 6-in. taping knives on each side. Build up each side, but not the center, with joint compound, and feather the edges with a beveled trowel.

When this coat is dry, check the seam again with a straightedge; if it is acceptable, lightly sand the seam and apply the final coat in the same way the other seams and outside corners were third-coated (see p. 89 for other ways to handle a butted seam).

To conceal a crowned seam, apply joint compound the width of two 6-in. taping knives on each side. Build them up while leaving only a thin layer of compound in the center.

sandpaper or sanding screen (see p. 47). Using light pressure, sand every seam to remove small ridges, bumps, unfeathered edges, small chunks, and trowel marks. Be careful not to sand down to the paper or mesh tape. The aim is not to sand out every last defect but just to make it easier to get the finish coat of joint compound as smooth as possible. (It helps to think of this step as a light "brushing" rather than sanding per se.)

There are two ways to apply the finish coat to the seams: with a taping knife (the conventional method) or with a paint roller (the faster method if you have a helper).

TAPING-KNIFE APPLICATION. Apply the compound over the entire seam with a 6-in. or wider taping knife, going slightly wider than the second coat. Next, remove most of the joint compound by pulling a 12-in. trowel firmly along the seam. Feather the edges one last time so that there are no thick or rough spots, and then take off any compound left on

---

■ WORK SAFE
■ WORK SMART
■ THINKING AHEAD

As you apply the third coat, note any areas that require additional feathering or filling. You must take care of them before you sand.

One way to apply the third coat of joint compound to a seam is with a wide taping knife.

A quicker alternative is to use a paint roller. Dilute the compound slightly for easier application.

the center of the seam. The thin layer of compound left fills in all imperfections, scratches, dents, air bubbles, and so on. The compound dries out a little as it is worked, so you can thin it with water as necessary for easier application.

PAINT-ROLLER APPLICATION. Thin the joint compound with a little water, and then use a ⅜-in. nap roller to apply it, again going just a little wider than the second coat. Then smooth and remove the compound with a 12-in. trowel in the same manner as described for the taping-knife application. I find that rolling works faster than applying the compound by knife, and if you attach a pole to the roller handle, it's easy to reach high seams. (Working with a long-handled paint roller also places less stress on your wrists and arms than applying the compound with a knife or trowel does.) One member of the crew can roll the compound on while another finishes the seam. This works especially well on ceilings.

Use a wide taping knife to remove and smooth the joint compound on the third coat. Feather the edges first, and then smooth the center.

General Guidelines for Applying the Third Coat

I recommend using a topping or an all-purpose drying-type compound for all third-coat applications. These compounds can be thinned with water and are easy to apply and sand smooth. Taping and setting-type compounds dry out too quickly on such a thin coat, and they are harder to sand.

Start the third coat by applying a thin layer of compound to the fasteners, and then move on to the seams and outside corners. Wherever taped areas intersect, smooth and blend them together, working both seams at the same time. Apply the finish coat to the inside corners after the intersecting joints are finished. When applying the third coat, keep the following points in mind:

- Make the finish coat just a little wider than the second coat.
- Keep all the seams smooth and the edges feathered.
- Fill all scratches and dents to create smooth seams with no trowel marks or air bubbles.

The third coat on a tapered-edge seam should be just a little wider than the second coat.

Taping Inside Corners

Inside corners are a little more difficult to tape than flat seams, because it can be tricky to get one side of the corner smooth without roughing up the other side. I prefer to use paper tape on inside corners; mesh tape doesn't hold a crease well, and it's easy to cut through the mesh with a taping knife (and easy to sand through it as well).

Generally, the paper tape is embedded in a layer of joint compound and then covered with one or two thin coats. One coat is usually enough, but sometimes two

For inside corners, apply the embedding coat of joint compound with a 4-in. taping knife.

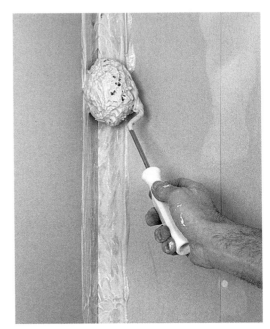

An alternative is to apply slightly diluted compound with a 4-in. corner roller.

are necessary (industry recommendations call for only one coat over inside corners).

First coat

The method I've used for years is to apply the undiluted compound (all-purpose or taping) right from the bucket with a 4-in. or 5-in. taping knife. Spread a layer about 4 in. wide and ⅛ in. thick or less into each edge of the corners. Make sure the entire inside corner is covered with compound, with no dry areas or unfilled gaps between the panels.

An alternative is to apply the compound with a 4-in. corner roller. You'll need to thin the compound with a little water, but in one swipe the roller gives you an even layer of compound on both sides of the corner. This method is quite a bit faster than using a taping knife.

Fold the tape along its crease and lightly press it into the corner every 12 in. or so, keeping the tape pulled tight as you go. Now embed the tape into the compound with a 4-in. or 5-in. taping knife, working on one side of the corner at a time.

It takes some practice to embed the tape on each side of the corner without accidentally pulling it loose, wrinkling it, or leaving too much joint compound underneath. Start with light trowel pressure to embed the tape, and then go over

Fold the pre-creased paper tape and position it in the corner. Pull it tight to avoid creating wrinkles when embedding it in the compound.

With the taping knife, press the tape in place one edge at a time. The first coat should be free of wrinkles and have feathered edges.

it a few more times with increased pressure to force out the excess joint compound. When you're finished, the first coat on the inside corners should be free of wrinkles and the edges of the compound should be feathered.

There is a tool that allows you to work on both sides of the inside corner simultaneously. This is a double-edged knife (see the center photo below), which was originally designed for finishing interior corners on veneer plaster jobs.

■ **WORK SAFE**
■ **WORK**
■ **THINKING AHEAD**

When taping an inside corner on a wall, work from top to bottom. When taping a long inside corner where the wall meets the ceiling, work from the center toward the ends.

A double-edged knife can be used to embed the tape in the corner. Firmly press the knife along the tape. A regular knife may be needed to feather the edges later.

If you use mesh tape on inside corners, apply it before the compound. Push the tape tight into the corner so it is centered and free of wrinkles.

Filling Large Gaps

Drywall isn't always hung perfectly. A problem you sometimes run into when taping inside corners, especially in older homes, is large gaps in the corners between panels. Gaps are typically caused by out-of-square or off-level walls or ceilings or by errors made during measuring.

Sometimes a gap can simply be filled with compound, but if it's wider than ½ in. or so, the compound will fall out. The best remedy for this problem is to first put a layer or two of self-adhesive mesh tape into the corner. When you apply the joint compound, the mesh holds it in place. The paper tape can then be positioned in the corner in the normal way.

Allow a little extra time for the corner to dry before applying the next coat of compound, because the extra-thick layer of joint compound can crack if it is second-coated too soon.

Use mesh tape to repair large gaps on inside corners.

After applying a layer or two of mesh tape to the corner, cover it with joint compound.

Finish by installing pre-creased paper tape.

A couple of firmly pressed passes from each direction are all it takes to embed the tape. Although the corner tool does a pretty good job of embedding the tape, the outer edges usually need to be feathered with a regular taping knife.

Second coat

When the first coat is thoroughly dry, use a 6-in. taping knife to apply a second coat of compound over the tape. Apply a thin layer to both sides of the corner (see the photo below). Once the compound is applied, pull the taping knife lightly along the inside edge on one side of the corner, keeping the blade almost flat against the wall. Smooth one side and then the other, being careful not to rough up the first side too much. Next, hold the knife a few inches out from the corner and feather the outside edge as you remove the excess joint compound. Do this on both sides of the corner. You'll probably need to go over each edge several times until they both look satisfactory. Again, this is not the final coat, so it isn't necessary to get the corner perfect. And it's okay if the paper shows through slightly in spots, as long as the taped surface is smooth.

Working both edges together takes some practice, and the taping knife must be held at just the right angle to avoid taking off or leaving on too much compound. Hold the knife almost flat against the wall and turn it out slightly so you don't remove too much compound or mark up the other side of the corner. A steady hand (and a light touch) is also helpful. If the third coat is applied in a similar fashion, very little sanding will be required.

ALTERNATIVE METHOD. Alternatively, you can tape one side at a time, allowing the first side to dry before taping the other. Each side must be carefully smoothed and feathered. With this

WORK SAFE
WORK SMART
THINKING AHEAD

For best results on inside corners, use a flexible 6-in. taping knife for the second coat.

Apply the second coat of compound to both sides of inside corners at the same time. Leave a thin coat that just covers the tape on one edge while trying not to disturb the opposite edge.

Some tapers prefer to apply compound to one side of an inside corner while applying the second coat to the seams between panels. Then they work on the other side of the corner while applying the third coat to the seams.

When you finish an inside corner one edge at a time, sand or scrap off any chunks of compound before applying the final coat to the opposite edge.

method, one side is taped as the job is second-coated and the other side is taped during the third coat. In other words, the completed corner ends up with only one coat of compound over the tape on each side, which means you need to apply the compound a little thicker. And because it's difficult to get one coat as smooth as two, a little extra sanding and light touching up with joint compound may be necessary later. This method is faster than double-coating each side, and it provides excellent results.

Third coat

If you're taping both sides of an inside corner at the same time, follow the procedure used for second-coating. Apply compound to both edges just a little wider than the second coat. Remove most of the joint compound, leaving only a thin layer to fill imperfections, and feather the edges. Fill in any voids in the very inside edge that may be left by the trowel or by joint compound shrinkage.

If you are finishing the inside corners by taping one edge at a time, finish the other edge now (the first edge was second-coated during the previous coat). Before taping the second edge, remove any chunks of dried compound in the corners by scraping them off with the taping knife. Be careful when sanding over exposed tape, because it may peel off or you may sand right through it.

Taping Outside Corners

For me, outside corners are a lot easier to tape than inside corners. There is no need to put any tape on the corner bead because it is nailed firmly in place (though you can tape the edge of metal corner bead to reduce corner cracking). In addition, there are usually no seams or gaps along the corner bead edge (if there are gaps, use joint tape).

First coat

Apply the first coat of joint compound to the corner bead as you tape seams and inside corners throughout the room. Just blend in the areas where seams or corners intersect the corner bead. Using a 5-in. or 6-in taping knife, cover the bead with joint compound and then press the compound into place with the edge of a beveled trowel or taping knife. Using the

raised outside edge of the corner bead as a screed, pull the trowel along the corner to cover the entire bead, except for the very outside edge. The inside edge of the joint compound should be feathered lower than the outside edge of the corner.

Second coat

Outside corners are easy to second-coat, because the raised outer edge of the corner bead acts as a screed for smoothing the compound. Apply the joint compound about 10 in. wide. Using a wide taping knife or a beveled trowel, apply pressure on the outside edge of the joint

Fire-Taping

Garages, utility rooms, and furnace rooms are often hung with fire-resistant drywall. In these nonliving areas, there's clearly no need to do three coals of taping, but you do have to apply one coat of joint tape and compound to achieve the desired fire rating. This single coat is commonly referred to as fire-taping.

Apply tape and one coat of compound to all seams and inside corners in the normal way; you don't have to tape the fastener heads. Outside corners require metal corner bead, which can be attached after you've finished taping, but the bead doesn't have to be taped. All gaps wider than 1/16 in. around pipes, overhead door brackets, and other protrusions should also be taped.

There is a self-adhesive fire-rated tape available that doesn't require a coat of joint compound to maintain its fire rating. It is an excellent choice for fire-taping gable ends and attics.

Only the tape-embedding coat is necessary when fire-taping garages and other nonliving areas.

Fire tape is a self-adhesive drywall tape that does not require joint compound to achieve its fire rating.

When applying the first coat to corner bead on an outside corner, spread the compound about 6 in. wide, keeping the raised bead clean and using it as a screed for a curved trowel or taping knife.

Use the raised outer edge of the bead as a screed while you smooth the sides and feather the edges.

compound and on the edge of the corner bead, holding the trowel almost flat against the compound. When you've finished the second coat, the outer raised edge should still be visible, the center should be smooth, and the edges should be feathered into the surface of the panel.

If a seam or an inside corner intersects an outside corner, both areas can be taped at the same time. Blend the areas together, filling and smoothing as necessary with a 6-in. or 12-in. taping knife. You need a very light touch at the intersection—just skim the surface with the edge of the knife to avoid marking up the other seam (see the bottom right photo on the facing page). Blending the two seams together when they are both wet

Apply a second coat of joint compound approximately 10 in. wide to each side of the outside corner.

Taped areas must be blended together wherever they intersect. Here the author is using a 12-in. taping knife to blend a seam with an outside corner.

can be tricky, so an alternative is to apply the second coat on the corner and allow it to dry before second-coating the intersecting seam.

Third coat

Apply the final coat of joint compound to the outside corners in the same way you final-coated the seams—with a 12-in. taping knife or a roller (see pp. 90 and 91). For the final coat, use either an all-purpose compound or a topping compound (my preference).

Apply a thin layer over the entire taped area, going 1 in. or so wider than the last coat. Feather the joint compound with a 12-in. taping knife. Remove most of the compound, leaving only enough to smooth the bead and feather the edge into the drywall surface.

A final check

After you've applied the final coat and before you start sanding, walk through each room to check that the taping job is satisfactory. Look over the seams and corners, checking for indentations, scratches, and areas where the tape shows through. Touch up any imperfections with a thin application of joint compound before going on to the finish-sanding process (see chapter 5). If anything requires special attention, such as a crack, a crowned seam, or an overcut outlet box, correct them before you begin sanding.

Skim Coating

If you follow the detailed instructions given up to this point for applying the first, second, and third coats, you'll achieve what the industry calls a Level 4 finish (see the appendix on p. 171). To take the job to a Level 5 finish, you need

One-Day Taping

The taping method described in this chapter can take anywhere from 48 to 72 hours to complete (from the application of the first coat to the thorough drying of the third coat). That's fine when you're working through an entire house, but there are times when it's desirable to do all the taping in one day. Fortunately, fast-drying setting-type compounds allow you to do just that.

Setting-type joint compounds harden chemically in anywhere from 20 or 30 minutes to 4 or 5 hours, depending on the type used. The compounds with the shortest setting times are ideal for one-day finishing. All three coats can be applied in the same day; if the taper is skilled enough, only two coats are necessary (the compound can be applied more heavily, since there is very little shrinkage as it sets up). Proper temperature, humidity, and airflow help complete the taping process in one day. The sequence of steps for one-day taping is as follows:

Accelerants can be added to setting-type compounds to make them set up faster, changing a 90-minute compound to a 20-minute product.

1. Embed the tape on seams and in corners, and cover any corner bead.

2. Apply the first coat to the fasteners.

3. Apply the second coat to all taped areas as soon as the first coat has set up.

Steps 1 through 3 should be complete by the middle of the working day. Use a compound that sets up in 2 hours or less, or mix the joint compound before you need it, to shorten the setting time after it is applied. (If that isn't fast enough for you, there are liquid and powder accelerants that speed up the setting time. They can turn a 90-minute compound into a 20-minute compound.)

4. After the second coat has hardened, apply the third coat. Use an all-purpose ready-mixed compound or a topping compound for this thin, final coat. These compounds are easier to work with and sand when the third coat is dry.

Levels of Drywall Finishing

If you're a professional, it's important to be as specific as possible when drawing up a contract for a drywalling job. I've seen contracts where the finished taping job is referred to in such vague terms as "taped to industry standards" or "taped to a workman-like finish."

This type of language can lead to problems. I know a taper who never received his final payment, because the owner wasn't satisfied with the finished taping job. It seems the owner did his final inspection with the help of a 500-watt halogen light, and he found a lot of little problems that he wanted fixed (never mind that the surface would never be exposed to that type of lighting again).

In an effort to prevent these types of misunderstandings, four major trade associations developed *Recommended Levels of Gypsum Board Finish*, a document that does a great job of explaining the levels of finishing and where specific finishes are best suited. (The relevant sections of this document are reproduced in the appendix on p. 171.)

To summarize, there are a number of factors to consider before you begin a taping job. These include:

- The degree of decorative treatment desired.
- The type and angle of surface lighting.
- The choice of paint and the method of application.
- The finish of the wall-covering material.

Factors that require a high level of finishing include:

- Critical lighting conditions.
- Gloss paint as a final finish.
- Thin wall coverings as a final finish.

Factors that require a lower level of finishing include:

- Textured surface as a final finish.
- Heavy-grade wall coverings as a final finish.

to apply a skim coat of compound over the entire drywall surface.

Skim coating is recommended if the surface will be highlighted by bright lights or if you plan to decorate the walls with high-gloss paint or a thin wall-covering (see the sidebar on p. 159). If you tape only the joints and fasteners, the porosity of the untaped paper surface will be different from that of the taped surface. In addition, the texture will be different; the taped surfaces will be smooth and fine, while the paper surface will be a little rougher. In areas that have been sanded lightly, the paper fibers will be raised. These differences are magnified by glossy paint.

Remodeling is another instance where you might consider skim coating drywall; for example, if you're trying to blend new drywall panels with an existing plaster surface. A skim coat helps minimize the textural differences between the surfaces and gives the appearance that the wall is all plaster.

To apply a skim coat, thin down a topping compound. The compound should not be runny, but it should be thin enough to trowel or roll on easily. For larger areas, I like to use a paint roller. Work a 30- to 40-sq.-ft. area at a time, so that the compound doesn't dry out

A skim coat provides the highest level of drywall finish, referred to as a Level 5 finish. Here the author is using a roller to apply the skim coat.

You can also apply the skim coat with a large taping knife.

Smooth the compound with a taping knife. As you work, the knife removes excess compound, leaving only a very thin layer. The finish should be perfectly smooth with few tool marks.

■ **WORK SAFE**
■ **WORK SMART**
■ **THINKING AHEAD**

When applying a skim coat, remember that the inside corners have already been coated, so there is no need to cover those areas again.

before you smooth it. Once you have the area covered with a thin coat, use a 12-in. taping knife to smooth the surface and remove some of the compound. The end result should be a smooth surface that is free of tool marks and ridges.

Mechanical Taping

In chapter 2, I gave a quick overview of the mechanical taping tools available. In this section, I'll briefly describe how each tool is used. If you want more information, many manufacturers offer classes on how to use their products. In some cases, you can rent the tools to get the feel for them and to see if you like them.

Don't expect these tools to turn you into a master taper overnight. They are quite heavy, and it will take some time to get used to them. In most cases, the taper must push the tool along the seam and use manual pressure to force the compound through the tool.

The basic tool is the automatic taper, which applies the tape and the proper

Mechanical vs. Hand Taping

The pros and cons of each taping method are listed below.

Mechanical Taping

■ Produces consistent uniform results.

■ Once mastered (usually only a day or two), is faster than hand taping, especially on larger jobs.

■ Often requires a class to learn proper use.

■ Requires only some of the tools. For example, you can use only boxes for finishing seams.

■ Requires tools that are quite expensive to rent or purchase; need to use them on a regular basis to offset the cost.

■ Requires less sanding than hand-taped jobs.

■ Doesn't require an entire set of tools for each person. Two or three people can stay busy with only one set.

Hand Taping

■ Is always necessary for difficult sections and areas that need special attention, such as crowned seams.

■ Takes quite a while to master.

■ Doesn't require a large investment to obtain a complete set of tools.

An automatic taper applies tape and joint compound simultaneously to a joint.

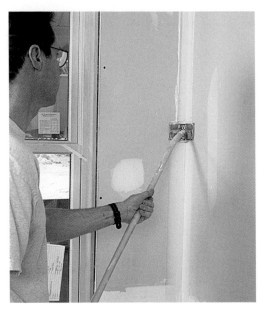

A corner finisher is designed to follow the corner roller. It removes excess compound left during the embedding process.

amount of joint compound simultaneously as the tool head is rolled along the seam or inside corner. After the tape and compound are applied, a corner roller is used to embed the tape in the inside corners. A 3-in. adjustable corner finisher is

used to clean and feather the compound after the corner roller embeds the tape. The corner finisher can also apply and smooth the finish coat on the inside corners; to do this, joint compound must flow into the finisher and then onto the corner.

After the tape and compound are applied to an inside corner with an automatic taper, embed the tape in the compound with a corner roller.

An angle box has a corner finisher attachment that is used to apply the final coat to an inside corner.

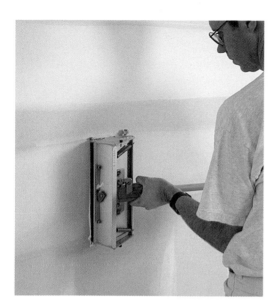

A flat box applies joint compound over taped seams; 7-in., 10-in., and 12-in. boxes are available.

A mud pump has a variety of nozzles for filling different taping tools.

An angle applicator is essentially a box attached to the corner finisher and filled with joint compound. The joint compound is forced out of the box and through the corner finisher, which in turn smooths and feathers the joint compound.

Flat boxes, also known as mud boxes, are used to apply and smooth joint compound over taped joints during the second and third coats. What I like most about them is the uniform results they produce. Flat boxes come in three widths—7 in., 10 in., and 12 in. I use a combination of 10-in. and 12-in. boxes. The box width determines the seam width, but you can adjust the blade trowel edge to achieve a precise crown on the compound.

Joint-compound loading pumps (or mud pumps) are designed for the many tools that need to be filled with joint compound. The pump comes with different attachments that fill the automatic taper and the mud boxes. The Universa™ Drywall Pump that I use is lightweight, stable, and easy to clean, and it has a reversible handle for left- or right-handed pumping.

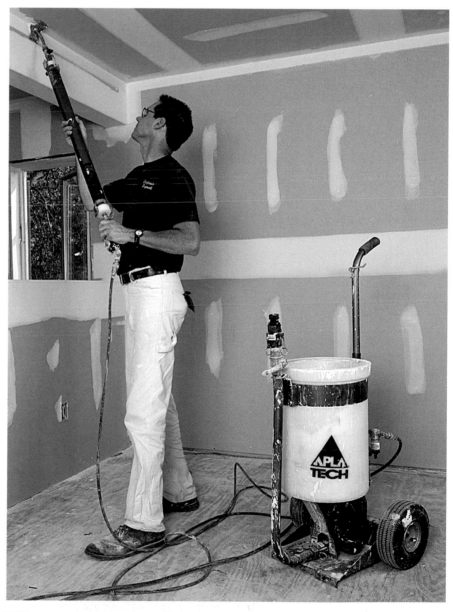

With some newer versions of mechanical tools, the compound is forced out of the tool head with air pressure rather than with manual pressure.

Taping Problems

As is probably obvious if you've read this far, the joints between panels can be a potential problem area. Some problems become apparent during taping, while others may not be noticeable until after the surface has been painted. In this section, I'll describe the most common problems, explain how to correct them, and suggest ways to avoid them in the first place.

Photographing

Photographing can occur when a wall or ceiling is coated with glossy paint (including high-gloss, semigloss, and satin finishes). Under direct natural light, the seams and strips of taped fasteners may still show through, even though they were taped and sanded correctly. This is because the panel surface and the taped joints have different porosities and textures.

This condition can be prevented by skim coating the entire surface before painting (see p. 99) or by applying a good-quality primer-sealer or a flat latex paint before applying the finish coat of paint (see chapter 8). If you notice photo-

graphing after the drywall has been painted, lightly sand the surface using 150-grit sandpaper, and then paint it with a good-quality flat latex paint before recoating it with the finish paint.

Crowned and concave seams

Crowned seams occur when taping compound is applied too heavily and the center of the seam is left higher than the surface of the panels. When light shines across the seams, they become quite obvious. If the seams have not been painted, the crowned areas can be sanded down with 120-grit or 150-grit paper. If they have already been painted, it is difficult to sand these areas, which is why it's important to look for crowned seams during the final check. However, the seams can be widened on each side of the crowned area. Feather the joint compound on each side, being careful not to raise the crowned area any higher. Check the joint with a straightedge when the compound is dry. If the crown has been corrected, apply a finish coat of compound before sanding.

Concave seams are the exact opposite of crowned seams. These defects, which appear as slight depressions along the taped seams when light shines across the joints, are usually the result of not applying the joint compound heavily enough during the second coat. Oversanding also causes concave seams. To correct the problem, reapply the second and third coats of joint compound.

Pitting

Pitting looks like a series of small pits or craters on the taped finish surface (see the right photo on the facing page). The pits are small air bubbles that were not properly filled or that were exposed during sanding. Air bubbles result from

Even after painting, seams and taped fasteners may be visible in certain light. This condition is called photographing.

overmixing or undermixing the joint compound. Small air bubbles may also appear on a wet surface if insufficient pressure is applied when smoothing the joint compound.

If a large number of air bubbles appear as you tape, keep going over the joints with the trowel, applying more pressure until most of the bubbles are gone. If you don't notice the bubbles until the surface has been painted, apply a thin finish coat over the problem areas. Then sand and prime the retaped areas before repainting.

Cracked and shrinking seams

If seams crack during the taping process, it's usually because the joint compound dried too quickly (often as a result of direct high heat or sunlight). As long as the tape and the joint compound are still solid, you can retape the cracked area. Make sure that the seam is thoroughly dry before you work on it, and use enough pressure to force the compound into the crack. If the tape is cracked or the compound is loose, you'll have to remove the effected areas. Cracked seams can be avoided by lowering the heat to increase the drying time. If the outside temperature is warm (above 80°F), close the windows so the airflow will not dry the compound too quickly.

Although it may sound contradictory, cracked seams may also result from joint compound drying too slowly. If a second coat is applied over a first coat that is still damp, the compound may shrink excessively. As the compound dries, cracks form where the compound is thickest. Any loose areas should be removed and filled with joint compound before retaping and finishing. To avoid this problem, make sure the building is heated more efficiently (to at least 60°F to 65°F) and keep the humidity low by

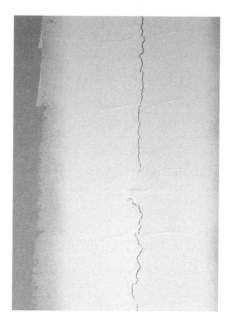

Cracked seams can occur when the taping compound dries too quickly or is applied too thickly.

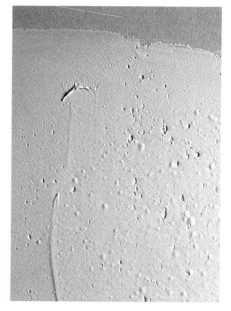

Pitting is caused when small air bubbles remain in the joint compound.

opening or closing windows, running fans, or raising the temperature. In addition, make sure the previous coat of joint compound is thoroughly dry before applying the next coat.

Shrinkage that appears along the center of taped seams after sanding is a related problem that is also caused by taping over joint compound that has not thoroughly dried. Remember that joint compound usually dries on the outside edges first, so a seam that appears dry may still be wet underneath. To correct the slightly recessed area caused by shrinkage, apply a layer of compound to fill the area, and then sand it lightly.

Bubbled tape

Bubbled or loose paper tape is caused by a poor bond between the tape and the joint compound. If the tape is not properly embedded in the compound, it can come loose and raise a bubble. The bubble may be a round spot only ½ in. in diameter, or it may run the entire length of a seam. Small bubbles can be cut out with a utility knife and retaped. For

This crack along the edge of a metal corner bead is the result of structural settling.

larger, loose areas, remove the entire section of tape and embed new tape, then apply a second and a third coat of joint compound. To avoid bubbled or loose tape, make sure that you apply a thick enough layer of joint compound before you embed the tape and apply enough pressure with the taping knife to embed it properly.

Popped nails and screws

Nail and screw pops don't usually show up until several months or years after the original taping job, but they do occasionally become apparent before painting. When sanding fasteners, a pole sander applies quite a bit of pressure against the panel. If a screw or nail has not pulled the panel tight against the framing, the pressure of the pole sander can push the panel tight and pop the fasteners, raising a pronounced bump on the surface or exposing the fastener head.

If fastener pops appear before you paint, refasten the panel while applying hand pressure next to the fastener to ensure that the panel is tight against the framing. The loose screws or nails should be reset or removed. Retape the fasteners with three thin coats of joint compound. If the drywall surface is damaged around the fastener, first place a piece of mesh tape over the damaged area. (For more on repairing fastener pops, see chapter 7.)

Cracked or loose corner bead

Sometimes you'll find a crack that looks as if someone has drawn a line with a pencil about 1 in. or so in from the corner along the length of the bead. Or the corner will appear wrinkled with some compound missing here and there. The corner bead can also be ridged out, creating an indentation where it meets the wall. These problems are more common with nail- or crimp-on metal beads and are usually the result of structural movement or settling.

To repair the crack, remove loose material, nail again where necessary, and apply a layer or two of joint compound to refinish the bead. Make sure that there is a ½-in. gap between the bead and the floor.

One way to help reduce cracking along the edge of a metal bead is to reinforce the border with paper tape.

CHAPTER 5

Sanding

F TAPING IS my favorite part of a drywalling job, I'd have to say that sanding is my least favorite. The dust makes the job unpleasant, and it is tedious, time-consuming, and fairly difficult work. It takes me almost as much time to sand and clean up as it does to apply one coat of joint compound (just under an hour for a typical 12-ft. by 12-ft. room). However, sanding is the final step in the drywalling process and, in my opinion, also the most important. It's your last chance before painting to turn a so-so taping job into a quality finished job.

Some tapers claim to be so skillful at taping that they don't need to sand at all. In my experience as a drywall contractor, however, I believe that a beautiful finished job requires at least some sanding after the final coat. (Depending on your taping ability, you may need to sand between coats as well, as discussed on p. 89.) Nevertheless, there are times when I have not sanded ceilings prior to texturing. In most light, those ceilings look just fine, but most customers aren't satisfied with a finished job that looks good in most light. They want a job that looks good all the time and in any light.

The goal of sanding is to remove excess joint compound, smooth out tool and lap marks, remove crowned areas, and feather the edges of compound to blend into untaped surfaces. Because you have to sand all taped seams, corners, and fastener heads, you end up going over a large percentage of the drywall surface. But if you take your time and have the right attitude (just keep in mind that once you're done you can start painting), the results are rewarding.

The joy of sanding.

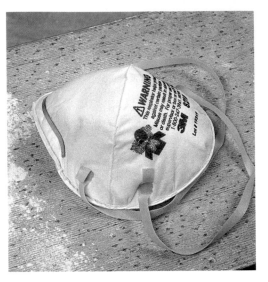

Use a dust mask that is approved for protection against nontoxic dust and mist. It should fit comfortably and form a tight seal around the edges.

▪ **WORK SAFE**
▪ **WORK SMART**
▪ **THINKING** AHEAD

Cover the front of kitchen cabinets and built-ins with plastic sheeting. Seal the entire perimeter of the sheeting with masking or painter's tape.

Getting Ready to Sand

Sanding drywall joint compound generates a lot of dust. Many of the ingredients in joint compound, such as talc, calcite, mica, gypsum, silica, and clay, can irritate your eyes, nose, throat, and respiratory tract. Protect yourself by ventilating the room and wearing a dust mask that is approved for protection against nontoxic dust and mist.

Make sure the mask fits snugly. When you breathe, air should not enter around the edges. (If air does get in, you'll notice white dust on your face around the edges of the mask when you take it off after sanding.) Change the filter or mask when breathing becomes difficult. It's also a good idea to wear a hat and a pair of safety goggles for protection against fine dust, especially when you're sanding overhead.

Attaching a sander to a shop vac can keep up to 95 percent of the sanding dust from becoming airborne. This greatly reduces the worker's exposure to dust and helps keep the area cleaner. Pole sanders also reduce your exposure to dust, since you stand farther away from the work surface.

You'll not only need to protect yourself while sanding but also the room you're working in (unless, of course, you're drywalling in new construction). On a remodeling job, remove

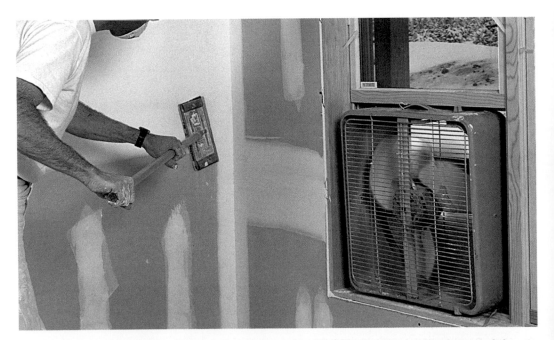

To pull dust out of a room, install a simple portable fan in a window and make sure it is blowing to the outside.

To protect areas from dust and debris, create a temporary wall with light plastic. The telescopic poles shown here hold the plastic against the ceiling and the floor.

all furnishings or cover them with drop cloths and plastic before drywalling. The fine dust generated during sanding can infiltrate the tiniest of cracks, so make sure you seal under all doors (including kitchen cabinets) to keep the dust from spreading. Seal the edges of the plastic with masking tape.

Try to contain the dust within the work area. Don't open all the windows, because that can create a draft that may actually push dust into other parts of the building. Instead, install a fan in a window to blow air out of the work area and get the dust moving in the right direction. In addition, hang plastic over doorways to isolate the rooms where you are working from other areas.

The Sanding Process

You could conceivably use power sanders to sand joint compound, but I do most of my sanding with hand tools (primarily a pole sander). An electric sander, such as a belt or disc sander, cuts through joint compound fast, but it is very hard to control and will almost certainly destroy the joint and dig up the drywall panels. Sanding is a two-step process. First, I use the pole sander to remove excess joint compound, such as marks left by taping tools, crowned areas where too much compound was applied, and intersecting joints that need blending. Then I do a final sanding with one or more hand tools.

Pole sanding

A pole sander fitted with a 120-grit sanding screen does an excellent job of smoothing the edges of seams. If you're sanding a nice, smooth taping job, you can use the finer 150-grit sandpaper or sanding screen. It doesn't cut through the joint compound as quickly as the 120 grit does, but it is gentler on drywall paper. It is important to sand only joint compound; avoid scuffing up the drywall face paper. The 150 grit works well with lightweight joint compounds or with topping compounds, which are slightly softer than all-purpose compound and

■ **WORK SAFE**
■ **WORK SMART**
■ **THINKING AHEAD**

To keep sanding dust isolated, wall off the area with plastic sheeting. Use telescopic poles to hold the plastic against the floor and ceiling to create a tight seal.

■ **WORK SAFE**
■ **WORK** SMART
■ **THINKING AHEAD**

Use a pole sander on ceilings and walls. It does a good job and is easy on your shoulders and arms.

Use a pole sander to blend the edges of seams and sand down any high spots. The 4-ft.-long handle allows plenty of leverage and keeps you at least an arm's length away from dusty surfaces.

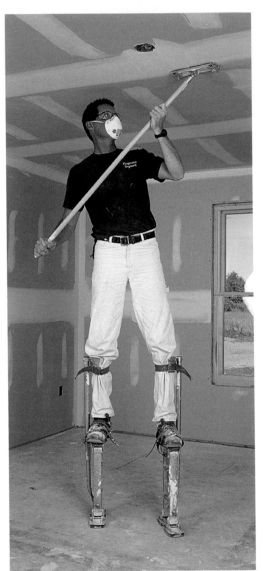

Working on stilts makes it easier to sand ceilings. Wear goggles or glasses to protect your eyes from dust.

scratch more easily with the coarser grits of sandpaper.

Using gentle, even pressure, push the pole sander along the seams and outside corners in the direction of the seam or corner. Keep the edges smooth, and sand down any high spots or chunks of joint compound on the seams. Run the pole sander over the entire taped area. Be especially careful when sanding inside corners, because there is only a thin layer of joint compound covering the paper tape. Blend in

the edges smoothly, and go along the inside edge only lightly with the pole sander. The inside edge will be finish sanded later with a hand sander, dry sanding sponge, or folded piece of sanding material.

Sand the screw or nail heads lightly in the direction of the strip of joint compound. Check the edges to make sure they are smooth. When sanding screws, you'll be putting pressure on the drywall around the screw head. If the screw has not properly pulled the drywall panel tight against the framing, it may pop loose under the pressure. The joint compound may come off the screw head, or you may see the drywall move in and out around the screw. To correct the problem, use a Phillips screwdriver and turn the screw until it is tight again. If it goes in too deep or does not tighten up, place another screw about 1½ in. away and then retape the area with three coats of joint compound.

Even though you can reach most ceilings with a pole sander, I prefer to work on stilts. Using the stilts gets me close to the surface of the ceiling, where I can better see the area that I am sanding. Also, most of the dust then settles away from my face instead of into it. (Wear safety goggles or glasses to help keep the dust out of your eyes.)

Don't try to remove every last defect with the pole sander—you may sand out the scratch or dent but in the process oversand the entire area. Some defects may need to be filled with joint compound and then sanded again later, so it's a good idea to keep a trowel with a small amount of joint compound handy. Fill in the defects as you go along, so they will not be overlooked.

If you notice a seam that is indented or slightly crowned, you may need to apply a third coat of joint compound, or in a worse case, a second and a third coat. A good way to check whether a seam is crowned too much is to hold the edge of a wide trowel across it (see the drawing below). If the trowel rocks more than 1/16 in. on either side of the center of the seam, you may want to widen the seam by feathering out the joint compound on each side, being careful not to add any to the crowned center. If the trowel indicates a recess of more than 1/16 in., fill in the seam with joint compound and then reapply a third coat.

Finish sanding

After all the taped surfaces have been sanded with a pole sander, I switch to a hand sander for the finish sanding. I also use a dry sanding sponge or a folded piece of sandpaper or sanding screen for the finish work. Before you get started, make sure you have adequate lighting.

Checking for Problem Seams

Hold the straight edge of a wide trowel across the seam to check for crowns and recesses.

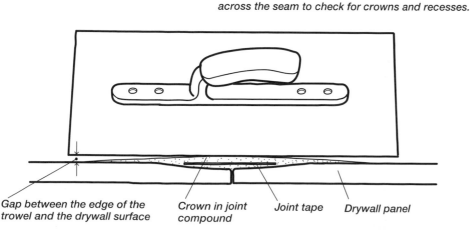

Gap between the edge of the trowel and the drywall surface

Crown in joint compound

Joint tape

Drywall panel

Oversanding

If you sand too much (a common problem with beginners) and expose the joint tape or damage the drywall face paper, you may have to apply the third coat of joint compound again. In more serious cases, you may need to reapply the second as well as the third coat.

If your sandpaper is too coarse, you may scratch the compound or drywall face paper. If you do, lightly sand the surface with a finer sandpaper or with a sanding screen (200 grit usually works well). If the scratches still show, apply a thin finish coat of compound and lightly sand it again when dry.

Some scratches and dents in the joint compound are too deep to remove without oversanding the entire area.

Oversanding can damage face paper and seams. This area will need another coat of joint compound.

Rather than trying to sand out the scratch, fill the area with a thin layer of joint compound and then sand it again after the compound has dried.

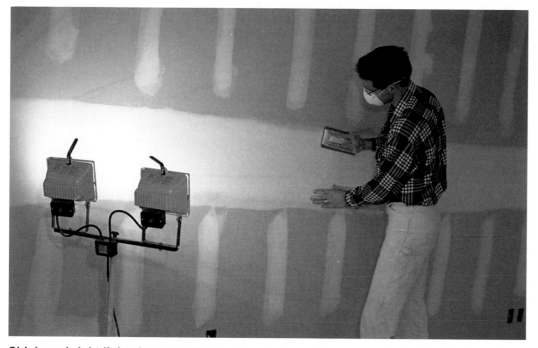

Shining a bright light along a wall helps illuminate problem areas during the final sanding.

A bright light shining along a wall or a ceiling helps highlight defects or problems you may not see with poor lighting or with natural lighting alone (see the photo above).

As you go over the compound with a hand sander, look and feel for defects that need to be sanded out.

Use a hand sander fitted with 150-grit or finer sandpaper or sanding screen and go over all the seams, corners, and fasteners. Look and feel for any defects. Lightly sand problem areas and any edges that are not feathered properly. Once again, remember not to oversand. If a defect is deep or if you sand through to the tape, repair the area with a thin coat of joint compound. Mark those areas with a pencil (a pen or marker bleeds through most paints) and resand them, if necessary.

Use a dry sanding sponge, a triangle-shaped sander, a folded piece of sandpaper, or a sanding screen to smooth small defects. I prefer to use a fine-grit dry sanding sponge to smooth both edges of an inside corner at the same time and to touch up the compound around an electrical outlet. Be careful around electrical boxes, because drywall face paper tears easily where it has been cut. I use a folded piece of sandpaper or a sanding screen to get into spots where other sanders can't reach and to prevent damaging the area around a defect.

■ **WORK SAFE**
■ **WORK SMART**
■ **THINKING AHEAD**

Use a triangle-shaped sander to get into tight spots. The thin edges clean up inside corners and the points get right into intersections.

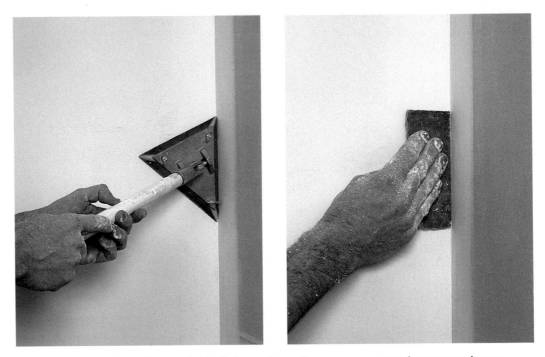

A triangle-shaped sander or a folded piece of sanding screen or sandpaper produces inside corners that are clean and straight.

Make sure you remove or sand hardened chunks of joint compound from taped seams and corners wherever they butt up against the floor, a window, or a door. These areas must be smooth so the trim or casing can lie flat against the wall. Use the corner of a taping knife to clean out hardened compound from electrical boxes (be careful not to cut the wires!).

General cleanup

After you've finished sanding, you can begin cleaning up. I use a wet/dry vacuum cleaner for this task, making sure to vacuum (or brush) out all the electrical boxes and remove dust from around window and door frames and along floor edges against walls. It's a real pain to have your brush or roller pick up dust or chunks of compound while painting, so do a thorough job.

In new construction, I recommend scraping hardened chunks of compound off the floor and then sweeping up the mess. A vacuum or a wet mop will pick up most of the remaining dust. If you've used drop cloths and plastic, carefully roll them up and shake them off outside. You'll probably still need to vacuum the floor or carpet, especially around the edges.

A fine-grit dry sanding sponge is used to sand inside edges of corners at the same time.

Wet Sanding

Occasionally, you may be working on a job where no dust at all is acceptable—for example, in an office building that contains sensitive computer equipment or in a home where a family member is allergic to dust particles. Even with careful covering and sealing of the work area, the fine dust that sanding creates is still going to get into unwanted areas.

Consider wet sanding, or sponging, for such cases. Because joint compound is water-soluble, you can blend the edges of taped areas and small defects with a wet sponge. When only a small touchup is required, an all-purpose household sponge or a smooth, soft cloth works effectively. For a larger wet sanding job, use a high-density polyurethane sponge made specifically for this purpose. The drywall sponge has small cells that retain water without excessive dripping.

To wet sand, dip the sponge in clean, cool water that is free of soap or additives. Wring out just enough water to eliminate dripping. Clean the sponge fre-

Dry Sanding vs. Wet Sanding

DRY SANDING

Advantages	Disadvantages
▪ Cuts down high spots easily	▪ Very dusty
▪ Most crowns and edges can be sanded out	▪ Easy to oversand
▪ Faster than wet sanding	▪ Need to wear a dust mask
▪ A pole sander can be used to reach high areas without a bench or scaffold	
▪ Excellent results after three coats of joint compound	

WET SANDING

Advantages	Disadvantages
▪ Not dusty	▪ Requires a better taping job
▪ Requires fewer tools	▪ Will not correct large defects
▪ Easier cleanup of work areas	▪ Just blends the area
▪ No need to wear a dust mask	▪ Slower than dry sanding

quently as you work. As you would when dry sanding, rub the sponge in the direction of the seam or corner. Avoid rubbing across a seam or into a corner too much, because this may cause rippling in the finish. Use as few strokes as possible, and be careful not to soak the joint compound. If the sponge is too wet, water may run down the walls, leaving visible streaks when dry. In addition, avoid excessively wetting the drywall paper, because it can rip easily when wet.

Although wet sanding is effective for blending the edges of taped seams and small defects, it doesn't work so well on ridges and larger chunks. Unlike sandpaper, which cuts down excess compound, a sponge just blends or rounds over an area. If you plan to wet sand, make sure you do an excellent taping job. After the third coat of joint compound is dry, examine the surface carefully, using a bright light to help highlight any problem areas. Apply a thin coat of joint compound to defective areas and allow it to dry before wet sanding.

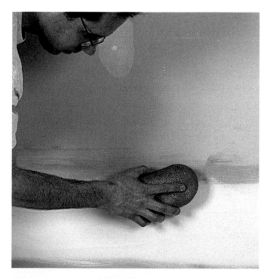

When wet sanding, use a wet (not dripping) sponge to smooth out taped areas. Rub the sponge back and forth in the direction of the seam, corner, or fastener strips.

▪ **WORK SAFE**
▪ **WORK**
▪ **THINKING AHEAD**

Wait until the finish coat of joint compound is dry before you start wet sanding. If you don't, the sponge may pull out joint compound in the wetter areas, and these defects will show after the joint compound is dry.

Dust-Free Sanders

For sanding jobs where you really need to keep dust to a minimum, try using a dust-free sander. This tool, which is relatively new to the market, is a pole or hand sander with an attachment that fits onto a wet/dry vacuum. It is used in exactly the same way as a regular pole or hand sander. The only difference is that most of the dust ends up in the vacuum cleaner, not on the floor. The model I use is designed as a pole sander, but you can remove the handle, reattach the hose, and use it as a hand sander as well.

This version of a dust-free sander eliminates debris by sucking it into a bucket of water.

The sanding head rotates on this tool. As you guide it along a seam, it does a good job of sanding the compound smooth.

CHAPTER 6

Special Installations

F ALL WALLS WERE straight and square with no butted seams and all corners were 90 degrees, drywalling would be a rather mechanical and predictable job. But, as those who are trying their hand at drywalling will soon find out, problem areas, unusual seams, and off-angle corners will present themselves sooner or later. These situations may be as simple as having to install extra fasteners to meet fire-code regulations or as complicated as having to bend drywall panels around a curved wall with a very tight radius.

In this chapter, I'll explain how to tape off-angle corners, archways, and curved walls; how to handle butt joints; how to hang drywall next to a tub or shower; and how to install multiple layers of drywall. In addition, I'll explain how to use resilient steel channel and how to work with cement board. Most of these special installations are really not much harder than hanging drywall on a straight wall or ceiling, as long as you understand how to approach them and use the right techniques and materials.

Flexible drywall and corner bead give a smart finish to a curved archway.

Tapes and beads are available for off-angle inside and outside corners to make finishing much easier. This tape comes in a roll; it has a slight beaded edge for outside corners and a nice crease for inside corners.

■ WORK SAFE
■ WORK
■ THINKING AHEAD

Be sure to remove any joint compound from the center of flexible beads. Get in the habit of checking the beads during each step of the taping process.

Off-Angle Corners

When a sloped ceiling meets a flat ceiling or a wall, the corner formed, which is usually much greater than 90 degrees, is known as an off-angle corner. It is much more difficult to keep standard paper tape straight and to achieve an even finish on an off-angle corner. In addition to being awkward, these types of corners are usually very visible, and they are subject to cracking due to structural movement or settling.

Fortunately, there are a number of tapes and beads tailor-made for these situations. My favorite bead is a vinyl product that adjusts to different angles and has a flexible center to accommodate normal structural movement or settling (see the photo below).

The center (creased area) of this bead should not receive a coat of joint compound. In fact, the very center should be completely clean after installation, so it is important to install the tapes as straight as possible. Begin by floating out any dips in the drywall with joint compound. After the compound dries, use a scrap piece of tape to mark along the tape's legs at both ends of the run. Snap a chalkline between the sets of marks. Apply an approved spray adhesive to the wall and to the back of the tape. Press the tape into position immediately, using the chalkline as a guide.

These beads can also be embedded in joint compound. Apply the compound to the drywall and roll the bead into place, centering it as you go. Sight along the inside edge and make adjustments, if necessary. Then press down on the legs with a taping knife. The legs will be concealed with joint compound blended into

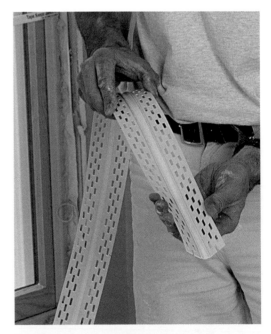

This inside corner bead has a rubber center that flexes and stretches should the building move.

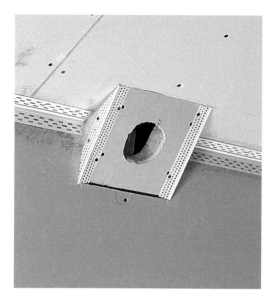

The bead is attached with spray-on contact cement and staples.

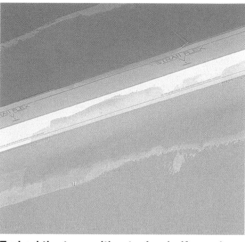

Embed the tape with a taping knife, and then sight down the tape and adjust it, if necessary. For finish coats, conceal the edges with compound, but keep the center crease free of compound.

the drywall, but the flexible center must remain free of compound.

There are similar products that are adjustable to different angles but don't have a flexible center. If they are vinyl, apply them in the same way as flexible bead; if they are not vinyl, embed them in compound. Use these beads only on

angles that are less likely to crack due to structural movement.

Beads are available for use on both inside and outside off-angle corners. For inside corners, install them by applying joint compound to the corner and pressing the bead into place with a taping knife. There is no need to apply com-

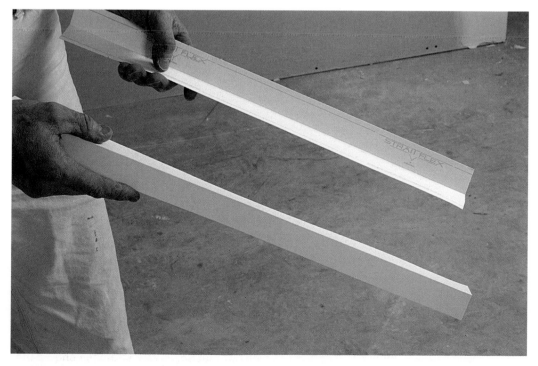

A closer look at an off-angle corner bead. Note the beaded edge for outside corners.

When properly taped and sanded, the sides of the joint are feathered into the drywall surface, but the center crease is free of compound. The result is a nice straight crease that provides excellent expansion control.

They come in standard lengths in metal, vinyl, or paper-covered metal or plastic and are attached and finished in the same way as 90-degree corners (see chapter 3). Keep the rounded edges as clean as possible during taping and sand any remaining compound off when dry.

Rounded corners technique

Before all of these new tapes and beads became available, I used the method described below for taping off-angle inside corners. To avoid crooked corners, I finished any corner that was 120 degrees or wider (and longer than 4 ft.) by "rounding" it slightly (see the drawing below). It is a good technique, and I still use it occasionally. Rounding makes the corner appear straight, even though it is slightly off, because there is no obvious interior angle.

pound to the center of the bead. When used as an outside corner, these beads should be finished like any other outside corner (see chapter 4). These products come in rolls, can be cut to length, and adjust to accommodate a wide range of angles.

Bullnose beads are also available for off-angle inside and outside corners.

As with regular inside corners, rounded corners can be finished with three coats of joint compound. I recommend using fiberglass-mesh tape combined with a setting-type joint compound for the first coat. First, cover the corner with the mesh tape, as shown in

Rounding an Inside Corner

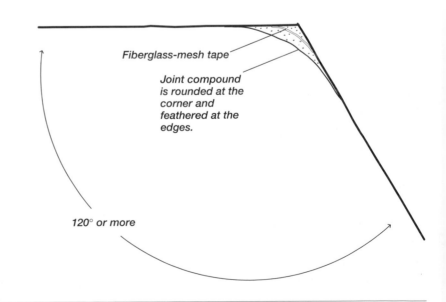

Fiberglass-mesh tape

Joint compound is rounded at the corner and feathered at the edges.

120° or more

the top photo at right. If there are large gaps between panels or damaged sections, apply an additional piece of mesh tape to cover those areas. Next, use a 6-in. taping knife to apply a thin coat of joint compound to each side of the corner, as shown in the bottom photo at right. At this stage, it's not necessary to cover the tape completely; a layer about ⅛ in. thick and 4 in. or 5 in. wide is sufficient.

Once you've applied the compound, pull the taping knife across the corner at a 90-degree angle (see the top left photo on p. 122). After you've gone across the corner in one direction, there will still be gaps and rough edges in the compound; to correct those areas, pull the knife across the corner in the opposite direction. Take your time, and don't apply too much pressure (very little joint compound should be removed if you're doing it right). As you pull the knife gently across the corner, feather the edges of the compound and slightly round the center. By now the tape should be completely covered and there should not be any large gaps or high ridges left by the knife.

For the second coat on a rounded corner, use a setting-type compound, an all-purpose compound, or a ready-mixed taping compound. I prefer to use a setting-type compound for this coat, because a pretty heavy layer of compound is left in the rounded area of the corner, which can result in excessive shrinkage if you use a drying type. Shrinkage can cause deep cracks that require taped reinforcement to correct.

Using a 6-in. knife, apply about the same amount of compound to each side of the corner as you did during the first coat. On this coat, use a 12-in. straight-handled trowel to round the compound (see the top right photo on p. 122). Pull the trowel across the corner in one direction and then in the opposite direction,

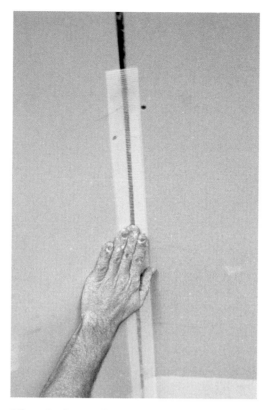

When taping an inside off-angle corner, use mesh tape to cover the joint.

Use a 6-in. taping knife to apply a thin layer of setting-type joint compound about 4 in. or 5 in. wide on each side of the joint.

There is a heavy buildup of compound in a rounded corner, so be sure to use a setting-type compound for the first two coats to resist cracking.

Pull the knife lightly across the corner in one direction for the length of the joint, and then pull the knife back across the corner in the opposite direction. The center of the joint should be filled and slightly rounded and the edges should be feathered.

Use a 12-in. knife to round the corners after applying the second coat in a manner similar to the first coat.

A paint roller works well for applying the third coat of joint compound to a rounded corner.

just as you did for the first coat. Once again, very little compound should be removed as the corner is rounded and the edges are feathered.

Before applying the third coat, lightly sand any high trowel marks and feather the edges with a pole sander and 120-grit sandpaper or sanding screen (be careful not to oversand or dig up the center areas). For the third coat, use a topping or an all-purpose ready-mixed compound. You can apply joint compound with a 6-in. or 12-in. knife, but I find that a roller works best, since it easily follows the curve of the rounded corner (see the photo at left). Cover the entire taped area with a thin layer of joint compound, widening each edge. Then use a 12-in. trowel to remove the compound, in much the same way that the third coat on a regular seam is finished (see p. 89). All trowel marks and

Smooth the compound with a 12-in. knife.

indentations should be filled, and only a thin film of compound should remain on the rest of the corner.

Curved Walls

Drywall can be formed to fit almost any curved surface, whether convex or concave. Depending on the radius of the curve, it can be applied wet or dry. The first curved surface I ever tried to drywall was a convex wall with a very short radius. (Walls with a short radius—32 in. or less—form a tight curve; walls with a longer radius—32 in. or more—form a gentler curve.) At that time, the only advice I'd been given was to wet a regular ½-in. drywall panel and allow it to sit for a while before hanging it. Given my lack of experience, it's not surprising that I

didn't have much luck with this job. I ended up having to cut the drywall, which I had wet on both sides, into narrow strips in order to get it to bend around the studs. After the narrow strips dried, I had to tape each seam and then skim-coat the entire surface.

Looking back, I realize what I did wrong. First, the wall was much too tightly curved to bend a ½-in. drywall panel around it. Second, I should not have wet both sides of the panel. Third, the studs were spaced too far apart for such a tight curve. If you are planning to attach drywall to a curved surface, here are a few important points to bear in mind:

- To avoid creating flat areas between studs, the framing should be closer together on curved walls than on straight walls. Maximum stud spacing is 9 in. o.c. for most curves; for really short radii, a maximum of 6 in. o.c. is recommended (see the chart on p. 125). Don't try to drywall an inside curve that has a radius less than 20 in. or an outside curve with one less than 15 in.; these curves are too tight, and the panels will break.

- Use ¼-in. flexible drywall for both inside (concave) and outside (convex) curves. Attach the drywall horizontally and place the screws a maximum of 12 in. o.c. Two layers of ¼-in. drywall are usually necessary for strength and to blend in with the ½-in. drywall used on straight sections of the wall. Apply one layer at a time, staggering the joints. If possible, avoid end joints butted on the curved surface of the wall.

- For curves with a tight radius (less than 32 in.), dampen the drywall so it can conform to the tight curve without breaking. Using a garden sprayer, a sponge, or a paint roller

WORK SAFE
WORK
THINKING AHEAD

One-quarter-in. flexible drywall is more flexible along its length. However, it's a good idea to hang it perpendicular to the framing, because it is easier to conceal the joints when taping with the curve.

■ **WORK SAFE**
■ **WORK SMART**
■ **THINKING AHEAD**

If you're using ¼-in. dry-wall on the inside of an archway, you may need two layers to blend in the sides and provide added strength.

When fastening drywall to a concave surface, gently and slowing push it into place. Begin fastening at the center, working toward each edge.

(see the top photo on p. 126), apply water to the side that will be compressed around the curve (i.e., the back of the panel on convex curves). For a ¼-in., 4×8 panel, use about 30 oz. of water (35 oz. for a ⅜-in. panel, 45 oz. for a ½-in. panel). Stack the panels with the wet surfaces facing each other and let them sit for at least one hour before you attach them. When the panels dry, they will return to their original hardness.

■ When attaching drywall to the outside of a curved wall, start at one end of the curve and fasten it to the studs as it forms around the bend (see the photo on the facing page). When drywalling the inside of a curved wall, start by attaching the panel at the center of the curve and fasten it to each stud as the panel forms out toward the edges.

■ When taping the seams on a curved wall, use either mesh tape or paper tape and apply three coats of joint compound in the usual manner. If the drywall is wet, allow enough time for it to dry thoroughly before taping.

Archways

Drywalling a curved archway is a process similar to that of drywalling a curved wall. As with curved walls, ¼-in. flexible drywall works best for short-radius archways (on gentler arches, use regular ¼-in. or ½-in. drywall). Cut the drywall to the desired width and approximate length. Starting at the center and working toward the edges, screw or nail the strip into place, as shown in the top photo on p. 127.

■ **WORK SAFE**
■ **WORK SMART**
■ **THINKING** AHEAD

Even if the radius of a curve is large enough to apply flexible drywall without wetting it, pre-bow the panels for easier installation. Follow the directions on p. 63.

Form ¼-in. flexible drywall to fit convex and concave surfaces.

Bending Drywall

DRY-BENDING REGULAR DRYWALL

Thickness	Minimum bending radii
¼ in.	3 ft.
⅜ in.	6 ft.
½ in.	12 ft.
⅝ in.	18 ft.

WET-BENDING REGULAR DRYWALL

Thickness	Minimum bending radii	Maximum stud spacing
¼ in.	2 ft.	6 in.
⅜ in.	3 ft.	8 in.
½ in.	4 ft.	12 in.

If you don't want to buy a whole sheet of ¼-in. flexible drywall just to do one archway, then you can use ½-in. regular drywall instead. In this case, score the back paper of the drywall strip at 1-in. intervals (or closer, if the curve is tight). As the strip is fastened into place around the arch, the back will separate at the cuts, allowing the drywall to conform to the shape of the curve (see the bottom right photo on the facing page). After the drywall has been attached to all sides of the archway, fasten corner bead to the outside edges.

There are a number of beads made specifically for arches. Vinyl beads are available in square-edge and bullnose configurations. There is even an archway bead that comes in a 100-ft. roll; it has a fibrous surface bonded to plastic tape. All

For tight curves, dampen the side of the panel that will be compressed.

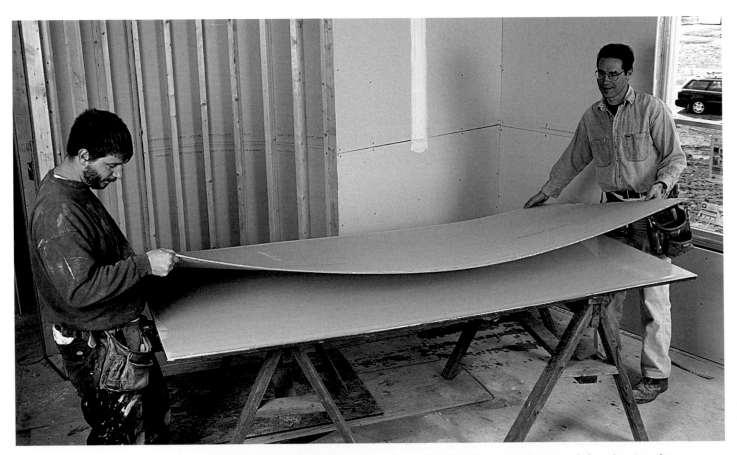

Place the wet sides of two drywall panels together and let them sit for about an hour before attaching them.

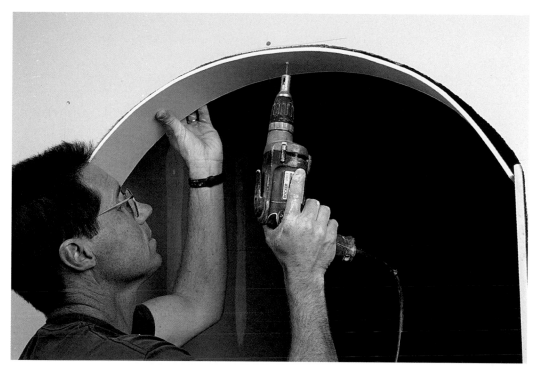

To drywall the inside of an archway, cut a strip of ¼-in. flexible drywall to width and fasten it into place, working from the center out.

Half-inch drywall will conform to an archway if the back paper is scored at regular intervals across its width.

As the scored drywall conforms to the curve of the arch, screw it into place.

Attach flexible corner bead around the arch. This particular type of bead is embedded in joint compound.

Cover the straight edges of the archway with regular bead.

of these archway beads have one thing in common: They are precut at 1-in. intervals along one side, so that they can flex to fit the outside curve of the arch. Start at one end of the archway, fastening the bead as you go and keeping it snug against the wall and curved surface (see the left photo above). If you can't find flexible corner bead, you can use tin snips to cut regular metal corner bead at 1-in. intervals along one side.

Once the corner bead has been fastened to the archway, attach a rigid, matching corner bead to the vertical sides of the opening (see the right photo above). Make sure the surfaces are flush and fit together evenly where the two corner beads butt together. Apply joint compound to the corner bead on the archway in the same manner as that for any corner bead.

Butted Seams

Throughout this book, I have stressed the importance of trying to avoid butted seams between the untapered ends of panels. If you have to use butted joints, make sure to keep them away from the center of the wall or ceiling and take time to feather the taped joints carefully. No matter how careful a job you do, however, the joints may still be visible after the room is painted. I'm embarrassed to say that I found this out when I returned to a job to take some photos for this book. What had looked like a perfect job on the day I finished had developed slight ridges at the center of the butted joints. The deformation, known in the trade as "ridging," was only visible in certain lighting, but it was enough to bother me.

Ridging

Building materials expand and contract as the temperature and humidity inside a building change. As the building materials move, tension builds up against the drywall panels. The tension is relieved as the panels bend outward, usually at a joint. Over time, the slight ridge becomes more stable and any additional movement will have no effect on the drywall.

Ridging can occur in regular tapered-edge seams, but it is much more common in butted end joints. After the ridging has stopped, typically in six months to a year, the ridged joint can be blended into the surrounding area by applying joint compound to both sides of the ridge and feathering it into the panel surface (see the discussion of crowned seams on p. 90). There are, however, a couple of ways to minimize ridging in the first place: by back-blocking with drywall or by using a back-blocking product.

BACK-BLOCKING is designed to minimize ridging by placing butt joints between framing members (see the drawing below). The drywall is hung perpendicular to the framing members, so that the butt ends can be reinforced along the back of each panel, behind the joint.

Begin by cutting two strips of drywall 3 in. wide by 4 ft. long, and nail them along the edge of the studs or joists that the joint will fall between. Keep the drywall strips set back from the framing sur-

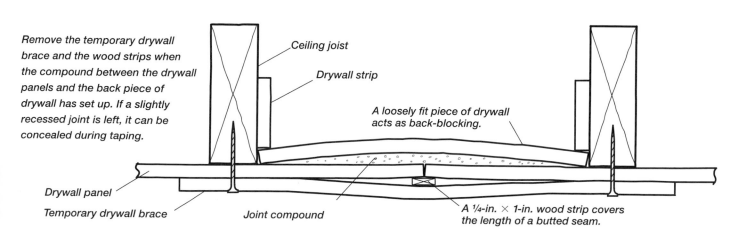

Back-Block with Drywall

Remove the temporary drywall brace and the wood strips when the compound between the drywall panels and the back piece of drywall has set up. If a slightly recessed joint is left, it can be concealed during taping.

Ceiling joist

Drywall strip

A loosely fit piece of drywall acts as back-blocking.

Drywall panel

Temporary drywall brace

Joint compound

A ¼-in. × 1-in. wood strip covers the length of a butted seam.

A back-blocking device creates a slight recess in butted seams. Here it is placed behind the first panel. Note that the joint falls between the framing.

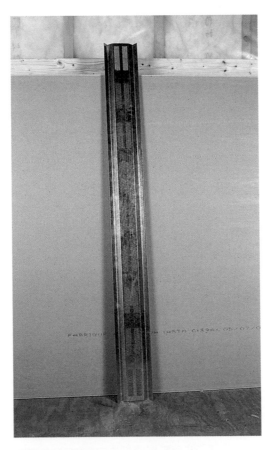

Different versions of back-blockers are available.

face about ⅛ in. more than the thickness of the drywall. Next, cut a piece of drywall 4 ft. long and slightly narrower than the width between the framing. Cover this narrow piece of drywall with joint compound, and use a notched trowel to leave beads of compound that are ½ in. high, ⅜ in. wide, and spaced ½ in. o.c. Toenail the piece in place between the studs with the joint compound facing out.

Now hang the drywall, centering the butted seam between the framing, and fasten it to the framing in the usual way. Attach the two panels so the butted joint fits snugly but not tightly. Next, place a ¼-in.-thick by 1-in.-wide strip of wood along the length of the joint to create a recess for taping. Hold the strip in place by fastening a temporary drywall brace over the joint, screwing it into place along the framing members on each side of the joint. The next day, remove the brace and the wood strip. The joint will be slightly recessed for easy finishing.

This method achieves excellent results, but it takes time and is quite complicated. I've also installed a plywood strip behind the butted seam. Again, it worked well, but it was not the most professional-looking device. Fortunately, Flat-Fast Inc. sells a back-blocking device. It is a wood strip that holds a series of metal legs.

To use it, hang the first drywall panel so the butted seam falls between two framing members. Now use drywall screws to attach the device along the back edge of the panel. Hang the abutting piece of drywall and secure its edge to the wood strip. Attaching the second panel puts pressure on the metal legs and causes the joint to bow in, creating a slight recess. The butted seam can then be finished in the same manner and with the same tools as those for a tapered-edge seam.

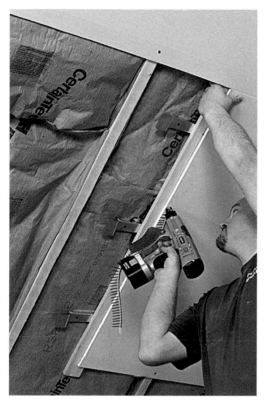

Screw the panel to the wood strip. Attach the next panel to the strip as well.

Butted seams are part of most drywalling jobs, so it is very important to properly conceal them.

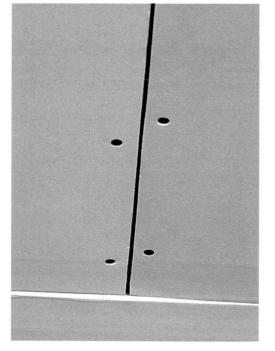

The design of the back-blocker pulls the seam in, creating a recess and making it easy to conceal. Since the joint floats between framing members, it is unlikely to crack or ridge.

The Benefits of Back-Blocking

▪ Finishes the butt seams flat and smooth, simplifying the installation of counters, trim, and cabinets.

▪ Produces finished seams that are the same width as beveled-edge seams.

▪ Takes less time and materials to finish them than typical butted seams.

▪ Allows the joint to float between the framing, virtually eliminating cracking and ridging.

▪ Eliminates callbacks.

■ **WORK SAFE**
■ **WORK** STEADY
■ **THINKING AHEAD**

Keep a plastic trowel or putty knife handy to remove joint compound from wood trim, fiberglass, and other easily scratched surfaces.

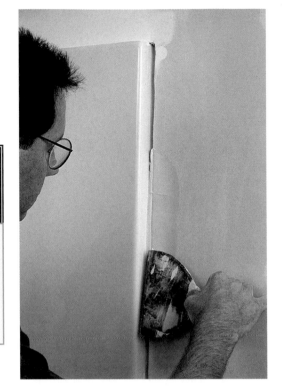

Before taping around a raised surface, such as a tub/shower unit, fill large gaps with joint compound and allow them to dry.

Apply fiberglass-mesh tape tight against the surface and cover it with a thin layer of compound.

■ **WORK SAFE**
■ **WORK** STEADY
■ **THINKING AHEAD**

On uneven framing, use resilient steel channel instead of wood furring. The spring action compensates better than wood, and it is usually less expensive.

Apply a second and third coat of compound, feathering the edges and keeping the abutting surface as free as possible of compound.

Flat Taping

When drywall is butted up against a tub/shower unit, trim work, or a wooden beam, it can be very time consuming to fit each panel perfectly and leave no gaps or broken edges. These areas can be taped for a quality finish.

Start by fitting the drywall as closely as possible to the abutting surface, and then fasten the drywall securely. To avoid a crack along the edge, make sure that the abutting surface is securely fastened. After attaching it properly, fill in any gaps wider than ¼ in. with joint compound and allow time for them to dry. Then attach fiberglass-mesh tape around the edges and apply a 4-in.-wide layer of joint compound with a taping knife. Smooth the layer of compound and feather the outside edges or, if it is close to a corner bead, fill to the outside edge of the bead, leaving enough compound over the tape to conceal it. Let the compound dry and apply a second and then a third coat, using the same techniques as those for taping one edge of an inside corner.

During each application of joint compound, try to keep the compound off the adjoining surface, especially if the surface is natural wood trim or a fiberglass shower unit. It's easy to scratch those surfaces with taping knives (or with sandpaper when sanding). Wash any joint compound from the surface with water and a sponge. If the joint compound is thick, dampen it with a wet sponge and gently remove the compound with a dull plastic trowel before sponging off the remainder.

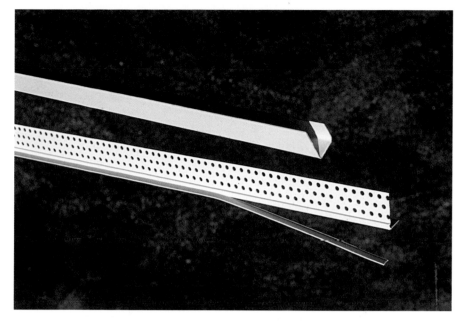

L-bead (bottom) is excellent for finishing drywall that abuts another surface, such as a tub or shower unit. This version has a tear-away strip of material that shields the abutting surface from joint compound and potential scratches. J-bead creates a finished edge for a drywall panel that will not be taped. A version that can be taped is also available.

Applying L-Bead

Flat taping works well, but it is difficult to prevent compound from getting on the adjoining surface. Rather than using flat tape, especially when wrapping window jambs, I use vinyl L-bead with a tear-away strip that acts as a shield to protect the abutting surface (see the top photo at right).

Attach the drywall, leaving it about ⅛ in. short so you can slip the leg of the bead between the drywall and the abutting surface. Secure the bead in place. The vinyl product that I use is simply stapled tight against the drywall surface. Apply two or three coats of compound to hide the bead. After sanding, remove the protective strip to reveal a nice clean surface. You can also use flat beads with protective strips when you can't wedge an L-bead between the surfaces or when you are working around an arched window.

Wrapping Doorways and Window Buildouts

Sometimes, windows and doors are recessed. Rather than install extension jambs or even trim, you can drywall these areas and install corner bead. Attach drywall to the recessed surfaces, making sure you use a sufficient number of fasteners, especially if you will be using a mud or glue-on bead. If you cut the drywall straight enough and smooth the edge, you won't need to tape against the window frame—either flat tape or install L-bead. If the gap is narrow enough, flexible caulk may be all that is necessary.

The jambs on windows and doors can be drywalled and beaded, eliminating the need for wooden extension jambs and casing.

When attaching the face layer of drywall in a multilayer application, apply a bead of adhesive at the location of the framing members.

Multilayer Applications

Double or multiple layers of drywall are sometimes required for increased fire resistance or for reduced sound penetration. You can secure all layers with fasteners in the standard manner, but a good alternative is to use adhesive to attach the outermost, or "face," layer. Using adhesive increases the strength of the structure and reduces the number of fasteners needed. Using drywall adhesives with single-layer applications was explained in chapter 3; the procedure is the same when applying the face layer of drywall in multilayer applications. Apply a ⅜-in. bead of adhesive over the location of each framing member (see the photo at left), and then fasten the panel around the perimeter and every 2 ft. in the center of the panel.

You can also use joint compound as an adhesive to attach the face layer (see the bottom photo on p. 134). Apply a strip of joint compound approximately

Joint compound can also be used as an adhesive when attaching the face layer of drywall.

When hanging drywall in two layers, the seams should not line up. Here we are attaching a second layer of drywall perpendicular to the first.

½ in. thick and 5 in. wide every 16 in. or 24 in. (depending on the framing spacing). Then use a notched trowel to groove the compound and leave beads of compound ⅜ in. wide by ½ in. high and spaced 1 in. apart. When using this method for wall applications, pre-bow the panels (with the bow facing in against the wall) and fasten only the edges. For ceilings, you'll also need a fastener in the center of the panel on each framing member.

These screws are used to attach drywall to drywall, giving the adhesive a chance to do its job.

If you use screws or nails to attach double or multiple layers of drywall, it's important to attach each layer with the correct number of fasteners. Never just tack the first layer or layers and fasten only the last layer correctly. Each layer is heavy and must be attached properly to prevent sags, loose panels, and popped nails or screws. In addition, make sure that the screws for each layer penetrate the framing at least the minimum depth of ⅝ in. for wood framing, ⅜ in. for metal framing (see the chart on p.33).

When installing double layers, it's best to attach the first layer parallel to the framing and the second layer perpendicular to the framing. This layout prevents having seams line up with each other, which would provide openings for fire or sound to pass through. However, it's often easier to attach each layer perpendicular to the framing, especially if the o.c. spacing of the framing is off. Just be careful to keep seams on the face layer away from seams on the underlying layer; the panels should be staggered so

Resilient Channel for Sound Attenuation

Sound penetrating through walls or ceilings can be a real problem in some homes and building complexes. Sound vibrations travel through the air and, when they meet a wall or ceiling, make the surface vibrate. On a wall, the vibration travels through the drywall into the framing and through the drywall on the other side. The vibration transmits the sound.

To reduce this type of sound penetration, walls and ceilings can be furred with a resilient channel, which is made of steel and screwed to the framing through an attachment flange. The channel floats the drywall away from the framing, thereby reducing the level of sound penetration caused by vibration. The channel should be attached perpendicular to the framing with screws (not nails) spaced 24 in. o.c.

For double-layer drywall applications, I recommend 16-in. o.c. spacing. Attach the drywall to the channel with the same type of fine-threaded screws used to attach drywall to steel framing. Two layers of drywall do a better job of stopping sound transmission than just a single panel. For single-layer applications, use ⅝-in. drywall rather than ½-in. panels.

Insulating the wall cavity also reduces the transmission of sound vibrations; acoustical insulation materials are available for this purpose. However, like water, sound waves will find a way through a wall if there are any gaps or openings. Areas to check include back-to-back electrical boxes, gaps around plumbing openings and ducts, cracks around door openings, and loose trim. To fill these gaps, use an acoustical sealant. Recessed medicine cabinets are another common problem, since they can transmit sound vibrations. If possible, switch to a surface-mounted cabinet.

To deaden sound and level ceilings, attach resilient steel channel perpendicular to the framing. Fasten the drywall to the channel with fine-threaded screws.

that the seams are at least 10 in. apart. On a ceiling, for example, start the first layer with a 24-in.-wide panel and the second layer with a 48-in.-wide panel. Use the longest lengths possible and make sure that any butted seams do not line up with butted seams on the first layer.

Installing Cement Board

Cement board, which is used in areas exposed to high water conditions (see p. 11), is cut with the score-and-snap method in much the same manner as that of drywall. Use a utility knife and a T-square or straightedge to cut through the glass mesh on one side. To break the panel at the cut, tap the back with a hammer as you apply pressure away from the cut. Then cut the back with a utility knife and snap the panel forward again.

Cement board dulls a utility knife very quickly, so change the blade often to

The author prefers using special screws such as these to attach cement board. It is a good idea to use adhesive as well.

Fastening for Fire Code

For single-layer applications of fire-resistant drywall to meet fire-code specifications, the panels must be correctly attached to the framing. Fasteners should be spaced no more than 8 in. apart along each framing member. Under normal conditions, the panels will stay in place with fasteners spaced 12 in. or 16 in. apart, but under the extreme conditions of a fire, the panels may come loose prematurely, thereby greatly reducing the fire rating of the application. (For more on fire-resistant drywall, see p. 8.)

Straight cuts in cement board are made using the score-and-snap technique.

Cutting Round Openings in Cement Board

To cut a round opening in cement board, mark the location of the opening on one side of the board. Drive a nail through the panel to help locate the opening on the back. Cut through the fiberglass mesh with a utility knife, and then gently tap the opening on the finish side with a hammer until the cutout falls away. Chip away any irregular edges with the blade side of a drywall hammer.

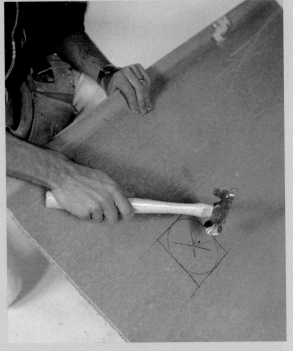

Mark the opening on both sides of the panel, using a nail to locate the center of the opening on the back.

Cut through the fiberglass mesh on both sides.

Tap around the edges of the opening with a hammer until the cutout breaks apart and falls out.

Galvanized-metal roofing nails can be used to attach cement board.

ensure smooth and easy cuts. A carbide-tipped knife keeps a sharp edge a lot longer. You can also make square and round cutouts in cement board with a utility knife and a hammer (see the sidebar on the facing page).

Cement board should be attached with special galvanized nails (not with drywall nails) or with screws designed for attaching cement board to either wood or steel framing. Galvanized nails used for metal roofing also work quite well (see the photo above). They have a large, flat head and are ringed for added holding strength.

Before attaching cement board, it's a good idea to apply construction adhesive to the studs. The adhesive adds strength to the structure, which is particularly important when tile is being applied over the cement board. The board is smooth on one side for adhesive applications and rough on the other side for thin-set mortar applications.

Working with Moisture-Resistant Drywall

Moisture-resistant drywall is different from regular drywall and has some specialized uses and attachment requirements.

■ Do not use moisture-resistant drywall for areas subjected to constant moisture, direct exposure to water, or continuous high humidity. Cement board or gypsum-core tile backer is recommended for those applications.

■ Space framing 16 in. o.c. for walls and 12 in. o.c. for ceilings.

■ Attach panels perpendicular to the framing.

■ Space fasteners 12 in. o.c.; if you are installing heavy tiles, space fasteners 8 in. o.c.

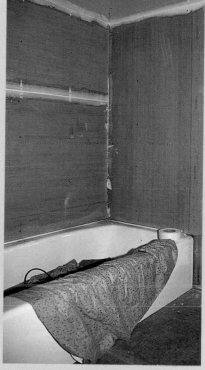

Moisture-resistant drywall (the green panel above) is often used in combination with cement board.

■ Coat all cut edges with a water-resistant tile adhesive or a waterproof caulking before applying joint compound. Place the drywall ¼ in. above a tub or shower lip. Be sure to coat the cut ends as described above.

■ Do not install moisture-resistant drywall over a vapor retarder if the wall will be finished with tile or some other impervious wall finish.

■ Use a setting-type compound to tape the seams. You can also use water-resistant tile mastic to skim-coat the drywall.

■ Use a nonabsorbent grout and sealant when finishing with tile.

■ Maintain the drywall by periodically sealing the tile; maintain the caulk around the edges and other openings as well.

Control Joints

There isn't a lot of need for control (expansion) joints in residential and light commercial drywall jobs, but they are required occasionally. The Gypsum Association recommends installing control joints wherever partition walls or ceilings transverse construction joints. An example of this is a stairway in a two-story house. If the drywall joint is anywhere near the transition from the first to the second floor, the seam will ridge out. And because these areas usually have an overhead light shining down along a

The center of the control joint expands and contracts as the structure moves. This joint has a tear-off strip, which keeps the center clean during installation.

wall, the seam is often difficult to conceal.

You could hang a panel to span the transition point, but ridging is still possible. That's why I like to use a control joint in those areas. The joint accommodates changes at the weakest point—in this case, the drywall seam. Leave a gap between panels, embed the joint in compound or glue or staple it in place. Be sure to leave the center of the joint clean so it can expand and contract as needed.

The center of the control joint remains free of joint compound.

Decorating with Drywall

Finished drywall is often thought of as just a smooth wall or ceiling. But over the past few years a number of products, including many of the beads discussed earlier, have helped make drywall a larger part of the decorating process. With L-beads (and even flexible L-beads), drywall can be layered for an endless array of designs. There is even drywall available with an embossed surface that, when finished, looks like wainscoting or a raised-panel ceiling.

To layer drywall, first hang the walls and ceiling in the conventional manner. Attach subsequent layers of drywall with screws and drywall adhesive. Because the drywall edges will be covered with L-bead, the drywall needs to be tight against the underlying layer for best results. In some areas, temporary screws may be needed until the adhesive sets up.

For a professional-looking job, it's important that you install the drywall layers and bead to a snapped line. I like to use vinyl L-bead to edge the drywall, because you can use spray adhesive and staples to hold it in place to the snapped line. Finish L-bead with two or three coats of joint compound in the same manner as for any corner bead.

This unique type of drywall has an embossed pattern. When installed, it creates a raised-panel design on walls and ceilings.

For a built-up effect, hang walls and ceilings in the conventional manner, and then use screws and adhesive to attach additional layers of drywall.

CHAPTER 7

Repairs

O MATTER HOW WELL you hang and tape drywall, there will inevitably come a time when you need to make some repairs. Drywall does not add much structural strength to a building, and it is not a rock-hard surface that can withstand repeated abuse. Some repairs are simply necessitated by the demands of daily life in a busy household, where doorknobs may strike against walls, pets may scratch surfaces, and children may playfully bang toys against anything in their path. Other repairs may be necessary if the drywall develops cracks or ridges as the building settles. Finally, remodeling often involves moving electrical outlets or light fixtures or closing off a window or a doorway.

Drywall repairs, when done properly, become a permanent and inconspicuous part of the wall or ceiling. Some repairs are simple and can be done with one or two thin coats of joint compound; others require additional framing and at least three coats of compound. The tools and taping techniques used for repair work are the same as those used for standard taping jobs.

Use a precut patch for openings around electrical boxes that were cut a little too large.

Popped Nails and Screws

Popped nails and screws are one of the most common drywall problems, and they are the easiest to repair. The problem occurs when the drywall is not fastened tightly against the framing, when the framing lumber shrinks or twists, or when an object strikes the wall. The joint compound comes loose from the fastener and

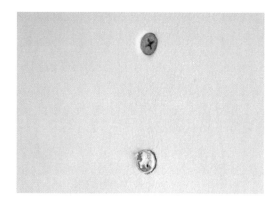

To repair a popped screw, place another screw 1½ in. away, and then remove or reset the popped screw.

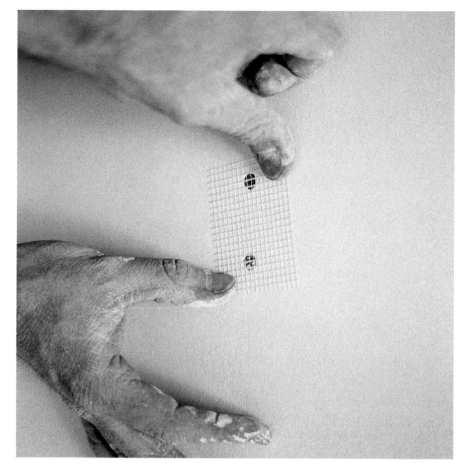

If there is any damage to the drywall surface, cover the screws with mesh tape before applying the joint compound.

pops off, exposing the fastener head or pushing out the joint tape. Fastener pops may appear soon after the wall or ceiling is finished, or they may become visible several years later.

Whatever the cause, the best remedy is to place another drywall screw about 1½ in. away, and then remove or reset the popped fastener. Apply hand pressure to the panel next to the area as you set the new screw. After the new screw or screws have been set, check the popped fastener and reset it again, if necessary (or simply remove it).

If the paper surface of the drywall has not been damaged, the fasteners can be finished with three coats of joint compound and some light sanding. If the paper surface has been torn or the core of the drywall has been damaged, remove the loose material, fill the gap with joint compound, and then apply a small piece of mesh tape to the damaged area. Cover the repair with three coats of joint compound.

Fastener depressions

These are areas around fastener heads where the joint compound is recessed below the surface of the panel. A depression occurs when not enough joint compound was applied during taping or when the fastener was driven too deeply

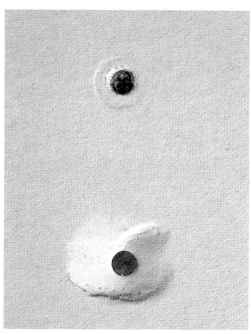

Both the nail and the screw shown here are set improperly, creating the potential for a depressed area around the fastener, even after applying three coats of joint compound.

To repair a fastener depression, place a drywall screw 1½ in. away, remove any loose material from around the original fastener, and then reset the fastener.

into the panel surface, damaging and weakening the panel's face paper and interior gypsum core. A fastener depression often isn't visible until after it has been painted.

To diagnose the problem, push firmly against the drywall panel next to the depression. If the panel is secure, you simply need to apply another coat or two of joint compound and then lightly resand the area to even out the depression. If the drywall moves in and out even a slight amount, the panel is damaged. To correct the problem, place a screw 1½ in. away from the original fastener, and then press against the panel again to check for any movement. If the panel is now tight, use a taping knife to remove any loose material from around the original fastener, and then reset the nail or screw by tapping it with a hammer or setting it deeper with a screwdriver. Cut a piece of fiberglass-mesh tape to cover the fasteners, retape the area with three coats of joint compound, and lightly sand it when dry.

Repairing Holes in Drywall

Holes in the drywall surface that result from long-term wear and tear range from small nail punctures to large gouges. The extent of the repair depends on the size of the hole. Nail holes, nicks, and small dents can just be covered with compound; small holes require paper or mesh for reinforcement; and larger holes require the use of furring strips to support the drywall patch.

Repairing small holes

A small nail hole (such as that left when a picture hung on a wall is repositioned) can usually be filled with just two or

The author likes to keep drywall repair kits handy. Shown here are precut patches for small holes, metal clips for larger areas, and precut patch kits for electrical outlets.

To repair a hole made by a doorknob-sized object, cover it with a self-adhesive metal and fiberglass repair patch or crisscross the hole with layers of mesh tape.

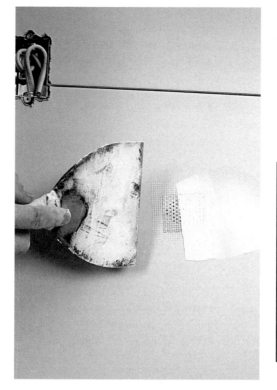

Apply joint compound to the patch. If using mesh tape, force the compound into the hole. Finish with two additional coats of joint compound.

> ■ **WORK SAFE**
> ■ **WORK SMART**
> ■ **THINKING AHEAD**
>
> If you can't fill a damaged area with one thin layer of joint compound or if the face paper is torn, apply mesh tape to reinforce the repair.

three coats of compound. Remove any loose material first and depress the area around the hole slightly with the handle of a utility knife.

Small holes or dents created when a blunt object, such as a doorknob, hits a wall can usually be repaired without major work. Completely cover the damaged area with mesh tape, crossing the tape over the hole (see the left photo above). Depending on the size of the hole, you may be able to fill it with joint compound before applying the tape. Next, apply joint compound over the tape with just enough trowel pressure to force compound through the tape (see the right photo above). Feather the edges of the compound and do not build up the center too much; otherwise, you'll create a bump that will be visible in cer-

tain lighting. Apply the second and third coats, feathering the area further and keeping the center even.

Repairing large holes

If an area is badly damaged, cut it back until you reach solid drywall. To make the repair, cut a drywall patch and use it as a template to form the damaged area into a square, rectangle, or circle (see the photos on p. 147). Once the damaged area is removed, the opening will probably be too large to repair with mesh tape and compound alone (as described on this page), because you need to attach the patch to something. To provide a fastening surface for the patch, use a furring strip (or strips) cut about 6 in. longer than the hole. Slide the furring into the hole and hold it in place with drywall

Repairing an Overcut Electrical Box

Electrical outlet-box and switch covers usually don't cover an area much larger then the box itself, so even a minor overcut may require some patching.

Before starting the repair, turn off the power to the box. Then apply hand pressure against the drywall panel next to the box. If the panel seems loose, place a screw in the framing member closest to the box. (The patch will be stronger if the drywall is solidly screwed in place around the electrical box.)

Fill large gaps with joint compound first, then cover the hole with mesh or paper tape and embed the tape in the joint compound. When the joint compound is dry, apply a thin second coat that just covers the tape and blend it into the surrounding area. For a small patch, you usually need only two coats before sanding. If, after sanding, you think it still needs another coat, apply a thin layer and resand it when dry.

If an outlet cover does not conceal the gap of an overcut electrical outlet box, the area must be patched.

Fill the gap with joint compound.

Cover the gap with a layer of mesh or paper tape.

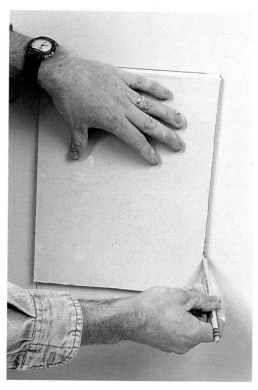

1. This looks like a great deal of damage, but if you use the right techniques, repairing a large hole isn't that difficult.

2. Cut a drywall patch a little larger than the opening. Hold the patch over the damaged area and trace its outline on the wall.

screws fastened through the panel and into the furring. Cut and shape the patch to fit the hole, and then screw the patch onto the furring.

Now you can tape the patch. First, fill in any large gaps with joint compound, and then cover the edges with fiberglass-mesh tape. Cover the tape with a thin layer of joint compound. Once again, be sure to feather the edges properly and be careful not to build up the patched area too much. Larger holes require at least three coats of joint compound to be concealed properly. Because the patch is secured to the panel and is a solid part of the drywall, it is unlikely to crack or come loose. For really large holes, furring strips won't be effective and you'll have to cut the drywall back to the nearest framing member and add cross framing, as when eliminating a door or window (see p. 152).

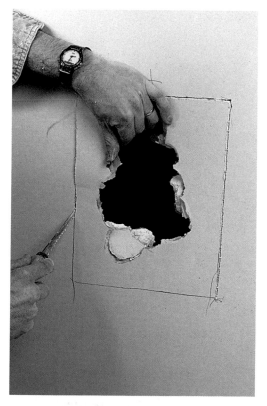

3. Use a utility saw to cut out the damaged area.

4. Slip furring strips into the squared-up hole and attach them to the drywall with screws.

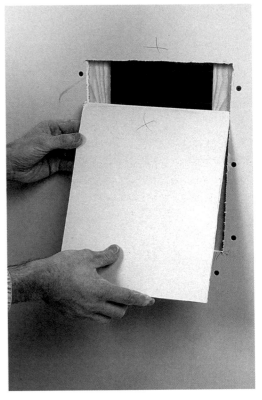

5. Position the drywall patch and screw it to the furring.

6. Fill gaps around the patch with joint compound, then cover the seams with mesh tape and a coat of joint compound.

7. Cover the entire patch with a second coat of joint compound, feathering the edges to avoid creating a bump.

Remodeling Repairs

During remodeling work, electrical outlet boxes, heating ducts, and other fixtures are often moved or eliminated, which means that the original hole must be covered and patched. You can install furring strips to support the patch, as described previously, or you can bevel the edges of the opening and the patch. When doors or windows are eliminated during remodeling, you'll need to add framing to the opening before patching it with drywall.

Eliminating an electrical box

When an electrical outlet is eliminated, the box may be removed or left in the wall. If the box is left in place, make sure there are no electrical wires inside (live electrical wires should be covered with a blank cover plate, not with drywall). To patch the area, start by trimming away any loose paper or drywall around the opening, and then bevel the outside edges with a utility knife. Next, cut a piece of drywall the same size as the opening (see the top photo at right), and bevel the back edges. Adjust the fit of the patch with a utility knife until the patch fits snugly into place without sticking out past the face of the drywall panel.

Apply a generous layer of joint compound to all edges of the patch (or hole), and then press the patch into place, making sure it is flush with the panel surface. To prevent the patch from cracking along the edges, apply some fiberglass-mesh tape or paper tape to the seams and embed the tape in joint compound. Once the compound is dry, cover the tape with a second coat and feather the edges into the drywall face. After the second coat is dry, lightly sand the area and apply a third coat, if necessary.

To patch an electrical box that is no longer in use, bevel the edges of the opening and the patch with a utility knife. The patch should fit snugly and set just a little lower than the face of the drywall.

Apply joint compound around the edges of the beveled hole or patch.

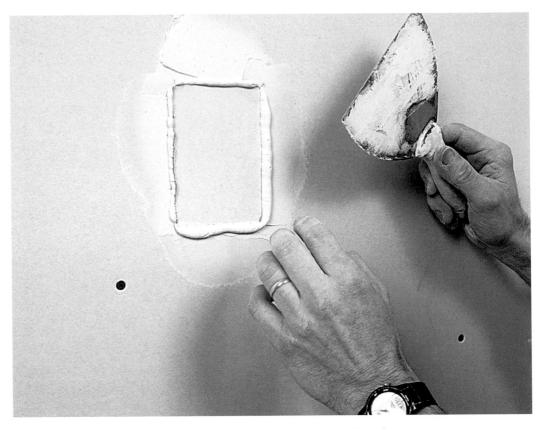

Push a patch into the compound until it is flush with the wall surface.

Another way to cover an electrical outlet opening is to create a paper flange around the edges of a drywall patch. Start by squaring up the hole and cut a drywall patch about 2 in. larger than the hole on all sides. Mark the dimensions on the back of the patch, subtracting about ¼ in. on all sides. Make sure the marks are in the center of the patch. Score along the marks (see the top left photo on the facing page). and carefully snap one edge at a time, making sure not to break the face paper. Peel the drywall off of the paper, leaving only the actual patch in place. Apply a thin layer of joint compound around the edges of the hole and press the patch into place. Use a taping knife to embed the paper flanges. Apply two more coats of joint compound to conceal the repair.

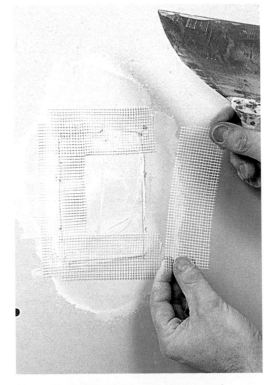

Cover the edges with mesh tape and conceal them with two or three coats of compound.

Another method of repairing a hole is to cut a patch with a paper flange. After scoring the patch on the back of the drywall, snap and peel off the waste material to create a plug for the hole and a paper flange to hold it in place.

A Quickie Repair

As you know, taping is a three- or four-stage process that sometimes requires waiting as long as 24 hours between steps. However, if you are making repairs, you usually don't want to wait any longer than necessary to complete the repair and move on to the next job.

One day, I was sanding an addition by myself. It was late in the day and I guess I was in a hurry to get home. I obviously wasn't thinking clearly, because as I disconnected the last cross brace on my pipe scaffold, the two side sections fell over. Both hit the walls. It took me a minute to get over the shock of seeing holes in my just finished walls. Then I headed to my truck for some setting compound, accelerant, and tape. I cut out the damaged areas and fit in the patches (as outlined on pp. 147 and 148), but instead of using an all-purpose compound, I used setting compound and added an accelerant (see One-Day Taping, p. 99). Less than half an hour later, I applied a skim coat of drying compound over the repaired area. The quality of the job was intact, and I didn't have to make extra trips back to the job to finish the repair.

Apply a thin layer of compound around the hole.

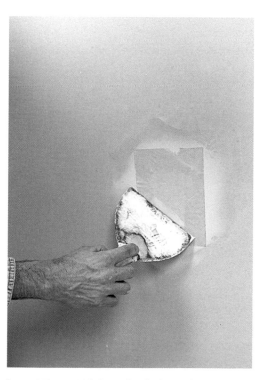

Insert the patch into the hole and embed the paper flaps. Apply one or two coats of compound, and the wall is as good as new.

Eliminating a door or window opening

For best results when eliminating a door or window opening, cover the entire wall with a new layer of drywall. However, that tactic is often not practical, and the more common approach is to patch just the opening. This type of large patch, though, has butted seams on all edges and is very difficult to hide unless you take great care to do the job properly.

The first step is to frame in the opening. Make sure that the framing lumber is straight, and install it a little bit behind the back of the drywall that is already in place. (If the wall is finished with plaster, just frame in the opening so that a ½-in.-thick piece of drywall will be flush or recessed slightly back from the finished wall surface.) Cut one piece of drywall to cover the opening. To avoid damaging the edges when screwing the patch in place, make sure the drywall doesn't fit too tightly (leave about ⅛ in. all around; see the left photo below). Fasten the drywall in place, and then cut away any high or loose edges with a utility knife or a rasp.

Since all the seams are butted, I recommend using paper tape and a setting-type compound for the first coat to provide additional strength. Apply a broad second coat, feathering the edges. Once the compound is dry, use a straightedge to check for ridges and concave areas. Do this again after the third coat. Four coats of joint compound are usually needed.

When a window has been removed, frame in the opening with studs. Hold the studs back from the surface of the wall just a little more than the thickness of the drywall.

Fill in the opening with one piece of drywall, leaving approximately ⅛-in. gap all around.

Treat all of the edges as butted seams, using paper tape for added strength.

Feather the edges as you apply the second, third, and, if necessary, fourth coat of joint compound.

An Ounce of Prevention

Roof trusses are often subject to upward arching, or uplift, of anywhere from ¼ in. to 2 in., with ½ in. being about average. Truss uplift is a complicated subject and not all trusses have this problem. But when it happens, the tape on the inside corners of interior partitions can crack, come loose, or pull away, giving the corner a rounded look.

To avoid this problem, do not attach drywall to the trusses that rest on partition walls. Use a drywall clip to attach the panel to the wall's top plate instead of to the rafter. An alternative is to float the ceiling edge and let the wall panel hold it up (as described on p. 62). Keep the first screw back on the truss approximately 18 in. This floating-corner method helps keep the corner intact during seasonal temperature fluctuations.

To prevent truss uplift, attach ceiling panels with drywall clips, as shown here, instead of screwing them to the ceiling joist. Install the first screw in the ceiling panel as much as 18 in. from the wall.

Cut along each side of the crack with a utility knife to form a V-groove.

Stress Cracks

Stress cracks, which typically occur above a doorway or window, are caused by structural movement or settling. If a crack occurs near a seam, the tape may blister or come loose. A stress crack can also occur where there is no joint in the drywall. It may run along the panel face, or it may go all the way through to the other side.

To repair a stress crack, first cut out any loose drywall tape or joint compound with a utility knife or the corner of a taping knife. The V-groove formed provides a wider area for filling with joint compound. Next, apply hand pressure around the crack to check for movement. If the panel moves in and out, fasten it to the framing member closest to the crack. This makes the drywall more solid and

If the drywall is loose around a crack, nail it along the closest framing member, and then cover the nails with tape.

less likely to crack again. Fill any large cracks with joint compound, and then cover it with mesh or paper tape. Smooth the area with two or three coats of compound and then sand it.

Water Damage

On drywall, water damage is usually confined to ceilings. Roof problems and leaky plumbing in an upstairs bathroom are two common causes of water damage. Usually, water runs along the top of the drywall until it finds a seam or corner. Once the joint compound on the seam or corner becomes wet enough, the water breaks through and runs down the wall or onto the floor. This type of leak does not usually cause extensive drywall damage, because the water found an exit and didn't pool on top of the drywall.

Before repairing the drywall, first fix the roof or the plumbing to prevent further damage. Next, remove any loose tape and joint compound. If the drywall has come loose, allow it to dry before refastening it. To prevent sagging, which is difficult to correct when reattaching a dried-out panel, prop up the drywall with a T-support or temporary furring strips. It's a good idea to go into the attic and remove and dry out any insulation that may be wet. Removing wet insulation allows the drywall to dry faster, and it may also prevent further damage. When the drywall is thoroughly dry, it will return to its original strength and can be refastened. Retape any damage using the techniques described in chapter 4.

To repair a water-stained ceiling, make sure that the damaged area is dry, and then remove any loose material.

Apply a coat of oil-based stain-killing paint over the stained area.

Mildew Damage

Under the right heat and humidity conditions, mildew can grow on any drywall surface. It usually occurs after the drywall has gotten wet. To correct a mildew problem, you must first eliminate the source of the moisture. If the problem occurs in a bathroom (the most common location), you may need to decrease the humidity in the room with an exhaust fan, a dehumidifier, or a better supply of heat.

Once the humidity problem has been corrected and the drywall has dried out thoroughly, wash off the mildew stain with bleach and water (¼ cup of bleach to 1 gal. of water). Repair any damaged areas and repaint the drywall with a mildew-resistant paint. Maintain low-humidity conditions to prevent mildew from recurring.

If a section of drywall has bowed excessively between the ceiling joists because it has soaked up too much water, the effected area will need to be removed and the opening patched in the same way as for large holes.

Water stains

Along with water damage, there will inevitably be some staining, and the stains will likely extend over a much larger area than the damage itself. Refasten or replace the damaged areas as described above. Then, before taping, seal all the stained areas with a good-quality stain-killing paint. I prefer to use an oil-based rather than a latex stain killer, because it better prevents water stains from bleeding through joint compound.

■ **WORK SAFE**
■ **WORK** SMART
■ **THINKING AHEAD**

Use oil-based stains rather than latex-based products to seal water stains. They do a better job.

After the stain-killing paint has dried, patch the damaged areas, then repaint the entire ceiling.

Once the paint is thoroughly dry, patch the damaged and repaired areas, blending them into the ceiling. Before repainting, check the ceiling for any stains that may have bled through and reseal them, if necessary.

Reducing Drywall Callbacks

Since this chapter deals with drywall repairs, it is fitting to end it with a list of ways to reduce drywall callbacks.

■ Use screws instead of nails to attach drywall. Screws should penetrate wood ⅝ in., metal ⅜ in.

■ Do not force panels into place; cut them for a loose fit.

■ Use the floating corner technique explained on p. 62.

■ Create a tighter bond by using panel adhesives, as explained on p. 61.

■ Make sure you use the appropriate compounds and tape (see chapter 2 for more information).

■ Whenever possible, install a back-blocking device for butted seams (see p. 129).

■ Select glue-on or tape-on corner beads, as well as special tapes and beads for off-angle corners.

■ Use control (expansion) joints, if necessary.

■ Use the appropriate grit of sandpaper or sanding screen and don't oversand.

CHAPTER 8

Decorating Drywall

ONCE ALL THE drywall work is done, the final step is to decorate the surface. Drywall can be finished with paint, textured coatings, or wall coverings. For satisfactory results, this step must be done properly. A poor finishing job can ruin even the most meticulous taping job.

Drywall can be painted or finished with a textured coating.

Painting

Painting is a little more complicated than just buying some cheap primer and rolling on a heavy coat of paint. Proper preparation makes an obvious difference. Surfaces should be dry, clean, sound, and free from oil or grease. Drywall manufacturers recommend dusting walls and ceilings prior to painting to remove the fine residue left from sanding, but in my experience there are no obvious benefits to this practice. I usually sand the walls lightly with fine sandpaper (200 grit works well) after the prime coat is dry. This light sanding removes small chunks of paint or drywall and knocks down raised fibers on the paper face, leaving a very smooth surface.

If you're working in a room with a finished floor, cover the floor with drop cloths to protect it from paint spatters; cover windows, doors, tubs, showers, and other fixtures with 1-mil plastic (known in the trade as "painter's plastic"). Make sure there is good air circulation in the room to help the paint dry properly. Wait the specified time before recoating.

The prime coat

It usually takes two coats of paint to finish drywall—one prime coat and one top coat. There's a confusing assortment of products that are advertised as prime coats, and it's important to understand the differences among them.

The terms "primer" and "sealer" are commonly used to refer to the first coat of paint applied before a top coat, but these two terms do not refer to the same product. A primer is mainly made of fillers and pigments that are designed to even out textural variations and provide a good adhesion surface for the finish paint. Primers often do not contain enough resin to even out the porosity of the different surfaces on taped drywall; when used as the first coat over drywall, photographing of the seams and fasteners may be a problem (see the sidebar at right).

Sealers have a high resin content, which is good for evening out the porosity of taped surfaces, but they usually cannot correct variations in surface textures. Again, photographing may result after top coats are applied over sealers. Primer-sealers, which combine the qualities of both products, do an adequate job as a prime coat, but they are not my first choice, either.

I find that I get the best results when I prime with a good-quality interior latex flat-finish wall paint. It provides good coverage as a prime coat and minimizes the problem of photographing. If I'm working on walls that will be painted a color other than white, I usually have the flat latex paint tinted to the same color as the top coat to avoid having to apply two top coats. Some manufacturers make a primer designed as a first coat for unfinished drywall. It works great and produces results very similar to those I obtain with flat paint.

How to Prevent Photographing

Chapter 4 discussed the problem of photographing, or taped seams and fasteners that are visible through paint in normal light. Photographing is always a concern if gloss paint (or even eggshell or satin finish) will be applied as a top coat. Even if you plan to coat with latex flat-finish paint, it's a good idea to prepare the drywall to even out the porosity and texture of the surface and the taped seams. There are two ways to do this: by skim-coating and by priming.

The best way to avoid the problem of photographing is to skim-coat the entire surface after the third coat of joint compound has dried (see p. 99). Skim-coating fills in any taping imperfections and smooths the paper surface. After the skim coat is complete, apply a good-quality primer-sealer or latex flat-finish wall paint before finishing with a top coat.

Although skim-coating is a time-consuming process, it is effective against photographing. It has become more widely used over the past few years; if left up to me, I would skim-coat any area that will be painted with high-gloss paint or that will receive a lot of direct light, such as a large, open ceiling.

At the very least, prime all taped surfaces with a good-quality interior latex flat-finish wall paint. Flat finishes have a very low sheen because of the fillers used to formulate the paint, and these fillers help even out the variations among the drywall face paper, the taped seams, and the fasteners.

Photographing, the term used to describe taped seams and fasteners that are still visible after painting, can be a problem if drywall isn't adequately primed.

The top coat

As with prime coats, there's a bewildering array of products that can be used as top coats. These include paints with flat, eggshell, satin, semigloss, gloss, and high-gloss finishes. Flat-finish paints are less prone to photographing, but they are harder to maintain. Gloss paints (including eggshell and satin finishes) are easier to wash than flat paints and are less likely to smudge and mark up; they are commonly used in bathrooms, kitchens, and other areas that need frequent cleaning. Gloss paints are primarily wall paints. They are seldom used on ceilings because photographing, which is often a problem with gloss paints, is more pronounced on the large exposed surfaces of a ceiling.

Gloss paints are harder to apply than flat paints and may require two coats for a quality finish. Roller marks or lapped areas that dried slightly before they were blended in become quite obvious on glossy surfaces. Whereas flat paint can be applied as a prime coat, gloss paint should not be applied directly over a taped drywall surface. Always apply a prime coat first.

Painting techniques

There are three ways to apply paint to a wall or ceiling: with a brush, a roller, or a sprayer. Brushes are used mainly for cut-

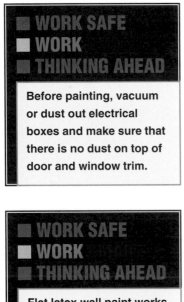

Rollers are available in a variety of nap thicknesses for applying different types of paint and for achieving different textured finishes.

ting in around trim and painting inside corners. Rollers are used to fill in large areas between brushed edges. Sprayers, which are used to paint an entire surface, are used primarily for large jobs in new construction.

ROLLING. Paint rollers come in a variety of widths and nap thicknesses. A 9-in.-wide roller, which is the most common size used, is excellent for painting small areas and narrow sections. Other roller widths include 12 in., 18 in., and 24 in. The larger widths work well for bigger jobs, not only because they cover more area with each stroke, but also because they leave fewer roller marks, which are more evident on large, open surfaces.

The nap refers to the thickness of the fibers on the roller. Nap thicknesses range from ⅛ in. to ½ in. for regular painting; thicker naps are available for applying and painting textured finishes (see the photo above). For best results, apply gloss paints with a ¼-in.-nap (or thinner) roller. If the nap is too thick, small bubbles will appear on the painted surface. These bubbles soon pop, but they usually leave a small mark or thin spot on the surface that is still evident when the paint dries.

■ WORK SAFE
■ WORK
■ THINKING AHEAD

Before painting, vacuum or dust out electrical boxes and make sure that there is no dust on top of door and window trim.

■ WORK SAFE
■ WORK
■ THINKING AHEAD

Flat latex wall paint works well as a primer for finishing drywall.

How to Prevent Yellowing

After the drywall has been taped and sanded, don't let it sit for too long before painting it. Timely painting is especially important when the surface will be exposed to direct sunlight for any length of time. Sunlight can cause the face paper to yellow or fade. If the face paper becomes too yellow, it may bleed through slightly when painted; the seams and fasteners will not bleed through, so the finish will look streaked. If the face paper has turned yellow, seal the drywall with a good-quality latex stain-killing paint before applying a latex flat-finish prime coat.

Using a roller with a too-thick nap (more than ¼ in.) to apply glossy paint can result in a pocked finish caused by air bubbles.

When painting with a roller, apply the prime coat parallel to the taped seams and the top coat perpendicular to the seams.

It's best to use a ⅜ in.-nap roller for flat paints. A roller with a shorter nap does not cover the surface as well, and a longer nap leaves a slight texture. Longer nap rollers (½ in. and greater) are used for light texturing and for painting textured surfaces.

When painting with a roller, always apply the final coat by rolling on the paint perpendicular to the taped seams. Each coat should be applied in the opposite direction to the one before it. For example, if two coats will be applied, the prime coat should be applied parallel to the seams and the final coat perpendicular to the seams. This system applies the paint more evenly and there is less chance of missing any spots. The roller flows over minor ridges or crowns along the seams, covering them with paint.

SPRAYING. If you use a sprayer to apply paint, I recommend using one that applies paint undiluted, like the model shown in the photos on p. 162. Paint is pumped directly from a 1- or 5-gal. pail and applied with a handheld spray gun that is fed through a hose.

Using a paint sprayer produces a certain amount of overspray and some airborne paint, so wear a respirator or a dust/mist mask. You'll also need to mask off walls and other areas that you don't want to paint. Follow the same procedure as you would when painting with a roller. Apply a prime coat and then a top coat. It may be tempting to spray on a good heavy coat of paint and be done with it, but the paint will just drip or run. For best results, apply thin, even coats (usually one prime and one top coat for flat paint, one prime and two top coats for gloss).

Spraying paint is much faster than rolling paint, mainly because paint is always available at the nozzle. Most rollers must be dipped into the roller pan repeatedly (although there are now rollers with an automatic feed). For finish painting, I prefer the look of paint that has been rolled on—it just seems to be more uniform and consistent. In order to

■ **WORK SAFE**
■ **WORK SMART**
■ **THINKING AHEAD**

Use painter's tape rather than masking tape to protect surfaces while rolling. Painter's tape is easier to apply, and it won't stick to previously painted areas. However, it's still important to remove the tape promptly.

Wear a respirator when using a paint sprayer; cover walls and other surfaces to protect them from overspray.

achieve both the speed of a sprayer and the finish of a roller, apply paint with a sprayer and then have a helper follow close behind and roll it out into a smooth, even finish (see the photo below).

Texturing

Decorating ceilings and walls with a textured finish is a very popular alternative to a flat, painted surface. Textured finishes, which can be produced in a wide variety of patterns, add beauty and contrast to drywall surfaces. They are

General Guidelines for Texturing

- ▪ Make sure the surface is clean and seal any stains. Texture a test area to check for bleed-through.

- ▪ Fill any cracks or holes in the surface and taped areas to create a smooth finish.

- ▪ Allow taped areas to dry completely before texturing.

- ▪ Use latex flat-finish wall paint as a prime coat to give the surface a low-luster appearance.

- ▪ Maintain a temperature of at least 55°F before, during, and after the texture is applied. Keep the area well ventilated while the texture is drying.

- ▪ For ceiling textures, make sure the joists' o.c. spacing meets maximum recommended guidelines to avoid potential sagging problems.

- ▪ Cover areas that are not going to be textured or clean up overspray promptly.

- ▪ Dull or roughen glossy surfaces to make the prime coat adhere better.

To save time and achieve a smooth, even finish, apply paint with a sprayer and then roll it out.

excellent at hiding minor surface imperfections and irregularities and, in their coarser forms, provide a certain degree of sound control.

There are a variety of textured finishes that can be created with a regular or an irregular pattern. The texture can be applied with a brush, roller, trowel, sprayer, or combination of these tools. The surface is primed before texturing and sometimes painted after texturing. Most of my work is done with sprayed-on textures, although I do occasionally apply textures by hand (see p. 169). The textures I use are easy to apply, dry fast, and have no odor.

Preparation

Applying textures reduces the amount of surface preparation required, but the surface must still be clean, dry, and sound. Textured finishes are only as good as the surfaces to which they are applied. Always apply a prime coat to new drywall and to any area where repairs have been made. If the surface is not new but has a clean, flat, painted surface, a prime coat is not necessary.

Seal any stains with an oil-based stain-killing paint. Apply texture to a small test area to check for stain bleed-through. Most textures have a high water content and take about 24 hours to dry. If a stain is not properly sealed, it will quickly bleed through and discolor the texture.

Ceilings that have yellowed after years of exposure to smoke need special preparation prior to texturing. The surfaces should be washed before any necessary repairs are made and then primed with latex flat-finish wall paint. As an extra precaution, texture a small test area to check for stain bleed-through. If the texture in the test area is still white after an hour or so, then it should be safe to texture the entire surface.

This simple compressor and handheld hopper, which apply textured finishes, are available at rental tool centers.

Water-based textures may cause ceiling drywall to sag between joists if the maximum o.c. spacing for joists has exceeded the requirements for the thickness of the drywall (see chapter 1). For example, ⅜-in. drywall is not recommended on ceilings, especially if the ceiling will be textured. If you're texturing ½-in. drywall, the spacing of the joists should not exceed 16 in. o.c.; for ⅝-in. drywall, the spacing can be up to 24 in. o.c. Both thicknesses of drywall should be attached perpendicular to the joists.

Application

Textures are usually applied with special spray equipment. For residential work, they are most commonly sprayed on with a handheld hopper (see the bottom photo on p. 165) and an air compressor. For commercial work, larger texturing machines feed the material through a hose and into a spray gun. Spray equipment can be rented.

Protecting Surfaces from Overspray

In new construction, overspray from the ceiling can be scraped off the walls with a wide trowel; when dry, it can be sanded before the walls are decorated. If a wall texture will be applied, very little sanding is necessary.

If the walls are already sanded or decorated, they must be protected from overspray. I like to use a 12-in.-wide strip of paper masked around the perimeter of the ceiling. A paper roller machine, which applies tape to the paper's edge as it is unrolled, works great for this purpose.

The tool and paper can be purchased at auto-body supply stores.

When a ceiling is sprayed, a certain amount of texture settles to the floor and lower walls. Protect floors with drop cloths and walls with 1-mil painter's plastic. Tuck and tape the plastic underneath the 12-in.-wide paper along the ceiling. Taking the time to cover everything before texturing makes for a quick and easy cleanup at the end of the job.

To protect walls and light fixtures from overspray, cover them with 12-in. strips of paper and masking tape.

Cover floors with drop cloths and walls with painter's plastic.

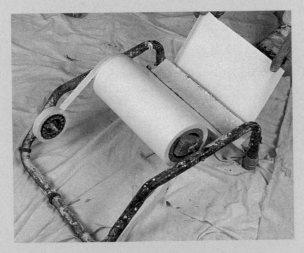

A paper roller machine applies tape to paper as the paper is unrolled.

The air, surface, and texture temperatures should all be at least 55°F during and after application. Once the texture has been applied, the room should be properly ventilated to help the texture dry. In an unventilated room, there is a greater risk of the drywall sagging as the moisture is absorbed into the drywall panels. Under very hot and dry conditions, the texture may dry too quickly, causing cracking and a poor bond.

Sprayed-on acoustical ceiling textures

Sprayed-on acoustical textures, often referred to as popcorn ceilings, are one of the most common and easiest to apply textures. The texture comes in a dry form containing solid particles made of either vermiculite (puffed mica) or polystyrene. The size of the particles determines the roughness of the texture; grades come in coarse, medium, and fine. You can vary the appearance of each grade by varying the density of the application; instructions for heavier applications are listed on the label. To achieve a heavy texture, two coats may be necessary. Apply the

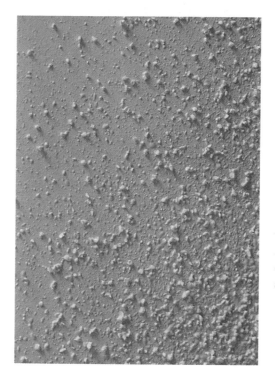

Popcorn ceiling textures are available in coarse, medium, and fine grades.

second coat of texture after the first coat is thoroughly dry.

After mixing the dry texture with the recommended amount of water, use a handheld hopper or spray gun to apply the material. Spray the texture by holding the applicator 2 ft. to 4 ft. away from the surface (see the photo below). Move

For a sparkle effect, blow glitter onto wet paint as it is applied.

Repairing Textured Surfaces

If a popcorn ceiling is damaged or badly stained, and it is determined that the best way to fix the ceiling is to retexture it (rather than just repainting it), scrape off the entire ceiling with a wide taping knife. Repair the damaged area, reprime it, and then spray on a new layer of texture. If the majority of the ceiling is still nice and white, you can repair and respray just the damaged areas. Scrape the texture off with a taping knife and feather the edges to avoid creating ridges that may show when the ceiling is retextured. To repair cracks in textured ceilings, scrape off the texture around the crack, patch the crack, and then prime and retexture the area. To touch up small damaged spots, mix a small amount of texture and apply it to the area with a paintbrush.

necessary to paint over the texture if it is stained or discolored for any reason.

Use a sprayer to apply latex paint to a popcorn ceiling. Because latex paint is water based, it will loosen the texture and damage the ceiling if it is applied with a roller or brush. If you want to paint the ceiling with a roller, use a flat oil-based paint with a long-nap roller (½ in. or more). Give a freshly textured popcorn ceiling 24 hours to dry before painting it. If you want to decorate with glitter, blow it onto the surface as you apply the paint.

Sprayed-on wall textures

Textures add a beautiful effect to walls; however, because walls are exposed to more wear and tear than ceilings, the texture must be durable and easy to wash and paint. Two very popular wall textures (which also make excellent ceiling textures) are orange-peel texture and knock-down texture. Each one is applied with the same spraying equipment that is used

the sprayer from side to side, applying a thin, even layer as you walk around the room. Then apply another layer, moving around the room in the opposite direction. Working this way helps avoid streaks or patterns that may result from applying the texture from a single direction. Finish the entire ceiling in one session. If you stop in the middle, a noticeable edge will be visible where the texture dried.

For an interesting decorative effect, popcorn ceilings are sometimes sprinkled with glitter to reflect light. The glitter is blown onto the ceiling when the texture is still wet. Glitter is available in a wide variety of colors and particle sizes.

PAINTING AND REPAIRING a popcorn ceiling is not usually necessary, since the texture is white and will stay white, unless it is exposed to smoke from cigarettes, kerosene heaters, or fireplaces. However, popcorn ceilings can be painted if a more durable and easier-to-clean surface is required (an unpainted popcorn ceiling is not washable) or if a different color is desired. It may also be

■ **WORK SAFE**
■ **WORK SMART**
■ **THINKING AHEAD**

When repairing a textured finish, respray or paint the entire ceiling to achieve an exact color match.

A hopper holds the texture before it is mixed with paint and applied to surfaces.

Spray cans of texture and texture-repair sprayers are convenient for touching up small damaged areas of textured finishes.

to apply popcorn ceilings. To vary the desired pattern, you simply adjust the size of the nozzle opening and the force of the air pressure.

You can buy special texturing compounds to create these textures, but you can achieve excellent results with an all-purpose joint compound that has been watered down and mixed thoroughly. (Setting-type compounds are not recommended because they can set up in the spraying equipment, making removal very difficult.)

AN ORANGE-PEEL TEXTURE is achieved by thinning joint compound with water. This makes it flow easily through the spraying equipment but, once applied, it stays in place without running or sagging. An orange-peel texture can be applied directly over a freshly taped drywall surface. However, if orange-peel texturing is part of a redecorating scheme, the surface should be smooth, solid, and first painted with flat-finish latex wall paint.

To create an orange-peel texture, spray thinned joint compound onto a surface.

Vary the appearance of an orange-peel texture by adjusting the air pressure of the compressor and the diameter of the spray nozzle.

Make a test area before finishing the entire surface. Hold the spray nozzle at a consistent distance from the wall (2 ft. to 3 ft. works well) and apply the texture evenly. Make sure the texture is consistent by mixing each batch of joint compound to the same thickness and keeping the airflow and nozzle opening at the same settings throughout the job.

A KNOCKDOWN TEXTURE is made from a coarser consistency compound than an orange-peel texture. Apply the material in the same way, wait about 10 minutes, and then use a large flat trowel with a curved blade to knock down the raised surface of the texture (see the photo below). Pull the trowel lightly along the surface, holding the blade almost flat and applying very little pressure. For best results, pull the

To create a knockdown texture, spray compound as you would for an orange-peel texture but use a coarser consistency.

Wait 10 minutes or so and then use a knife similar to the one shown here to smooth out the tops of the texture. Smooth "knockdown" in one direction only. It is usually best to work perpendicular to drywall seams.

Hand-applied textures

In addition to sprayed-on textures, there are many textures that can be applied by hand. Some of these textures have repeating patterns, which require a very steady hand to perfect. I have better luck with hand-applied textures that have a nice, uniform finish or intentional irregularities. The textures discussed here, which can be created with texturing compounds, all-purpose compounds, or setting-type compounds, are simple to apply and easy to maintain.

ROLLER TEXTURES are made by watering down joint compound to a consistency that will hold its shape and not run or sag when rolled onto the drywall surface. Use a short-nap roller (½ in. or less) and apply the compound as evenly as possible to the entire surface. Let the compound dry for 10 minutes or until the surface looks dull. Go over the surface again with the roller, leaving the desired textural appearance.

KNOCKDOWN ROLLER FINISHES are achieved in the same way as roller textures. However, the texture is then flattened with a large, flat, curved-blade trowel. Hold the trowel almost flat against the surface and use very little pressure as you pull it along in the same direction as the rolled-on texture.

HAND-TROWEL FINISHES are best achieved with undiluted joint compound or a texturing material. Apply a thin layer of compound to the entire surface in an irregular, random design using a 6-in. taping knife. The thickness of the compound should vary from some areas that are bare to areas that are ⅛ in. or so thick. Trowel marks, ridges, and low areas are desirable when creating this finish.

Once dry, all of these hand-applied textures should be coated with a good-

I like to paint the ceiling white before applying the texture to obtain a subtle contrast between the slightly different colors.

trowel perpendicular to the drywall seams and in only one direction.

Always prime the surface before applying a knockdown texture. The primer equalizes the absorption rates between the drywall and the taped areas. If you don't prime, the texture will dry faster on the taped surfaces. When you knock down the finish, the drier areas will not smooth out as much as the wetter ones, resulting in a texture that highlights the taped areas. If the surface is irregular and wavy, I don't recommend applying a knockdown texture, because the trowel will just hit the high areas and leave the low areas untouched, resulting in a spotty appearance.

Once orange-peel and knockdown textures are dry, they should be painted so the surface will be washable and more durable. These textured finishes can be applied to ceilings as well as walls.

The left side of this photo shows a roller texture. The right side shows the roller texture after it has been knocked down with a wide, flat trowel.

Create a hand-trowel finish by applying undiluted joint compound with a taping knife.

quality paint for easy maintenance and a more durable finish. Usually one coat of paint is sufficient to cover the surface.

Wall Coverings

Drywall is an excellent surface for all types of wall coverings, including regular wallpaper, fabric-backed wallpaper, and vinyl-paper-backed cloth. The surface should be sound, as smooth as possible, and free of peeling paint or plaster. If the surface is rough and loose, the wall covering will also be rough and loose, and it will not adhere securely. Thinner, shinier coverings require a smoother finished wall because they hide very few blemishes. Heavier wall coverings do not require nearly as perfect a finish. Also keep in mind that wall coverings are applied wet, so it is important that stains be sealed properly. Otherwise, moisture from the wall covering's adhesive may cause the stain to bleed through.

Preparation

For most wall coverings, you'll need to prepare the drywall with three coats of joint compound and then sand it smooth. Then apply a prime coat of latex flat wall paint. Once the paint is completely dry, apply a good-quality primer-sizer. This is a water-based product that serves a number of purposes. It helps wall coverings bond to surfaces (even to glossy or vinyl-covered ones), it prevents underlying colors from showing through thin wallpapers, and it minimizes damage to drywall when the wall covering is removed.

Appendix

Recommended Levels of Gypsum Board Finish

In an effort to prevent misunderstandings about the quality of drywall finishing, four major trade associations developed a document that does a great job of explaining the levels of finishing and where a specific finish would be best suited. Known as *Recommended Levels of Gypsum Board Finish*, it was developed by the Association of the Walls and Ceilings Industries International, Ceiling Interior Systems Construction Association, Gypsum Association, and Painting and Decorating Contractors of America.

The following information is taken from the document GA-214-96:

Level 0

No taping, finishing, or accessories required.
This level of finish may be useful in temporary construction or whenever the final decoration has not been determined.

Level 1

All joints and interior angles shall have tape set in joint compound. Surface shall be free of excess joint compound. Tool marks and ridges are acceptable.
Frequently specified in plenum areas above ceilings, in attics, in areas where the assembly would generally be concealed, in a building's service corridors, and in other areas not normally open to public view. Accessories are optional at specifier discretion in corridors and other areas with pedestrian traffic.

Some degree of sound and smoke control is provided: In some geographic areas this level is referred to as *fire taping*. Where fire-resistance rating is required for the gypsum board assembly, details of construction shall be in accordance with reports of fire tests of assemblies that have met the fire-rating requirement. Tape and fastener heads need not be covered with joint compound.

Level 2

All joints and interior angles shall have tape embedded in joint compound and wiped with a joint knife with a thin coating of joint compound left over all joints and interior angles. Fastener heads and accessories shall be covered with a coat of joint compound. Surface shall be free of excess joint compound. Tool marks and ridges are acceptable. Joint compound applied over the body of the tape at the time of tape embodiment shall be considered a separate coat of joint compound and shall satisfy the conditions of this level.

Specified where water-resistant gypsum backing board (ASTM C 630) is used as a substrate for tile; may be specified in garages, warehouse storage, or other similar areas where surface appearance is not of primary concern.

Level 3

All joints and interior angles shall have tape embedded in joint compound and one additional coat of joint compound applied over all joints and interior angles. Fastener heads and accessories shall be covered with two separate coats of joint compound. All joint compound shall be smooth and free of tool marks and ridges. Note: It is recommended that the prepared surface be coated with a drywall primer prior to the application of final finishes. See painting/wallcovering specification in this regard.

Typically specified in appearance areas that are to receive heavy- or medium-texture (spray- or hand-applied) finish before final painting, or where heavy-grade wallcoverings are to be applied as the final decoration. This level of finish is not recommended where smooth-painted surfaces of light to medium wallcoverings are specified.

Level 4

All joints and interior angles shall have tape embedded in joint compound and two separate coats of joint compound applied over all flat joints and one separate coat of joint compound applied over interior angles. Fastener heads and accessories shall be covered with three separate coats of joint compound. All joint compound shall be smooth and free of tool marks and ridges. Note: It is recommended that the prepared surface be coated with a drywall primer prior to the application of final finishes. See painting/wall covering specification in this regard.

This level should be specified where flat paints, light textures, or light to medium wallcoverings are to be applied.

In critical lighting areas, flat paints applied over light textures tend to reduce joint photographing. Gloss, semigloss, and enamel paints are not recommended for use over this level of finish.

The weight, texture, and sheen level of wallcoverings applied over this level of finish should be carefully evaluated. Joints and fasteners must be adequately concealed if the wallcovering material is lightweight, contains limited pattern, or has a gloss finish, or if any combination of these finishes is present. Unbacked vinyl wallcoverings are not recommended over this level of finish.

Level 5:

All joints and interior angles shall have tape embedded in joint compound, two separate coats of joint compound applied over all flat joints, and one separate coat of joint compound applied over interior angles. Fastener heads and accessories shall be covered with three separate coats of joint compound. A thin skim coat of joint compound or material manufactured especially for this purpose shall be applied to the entire surface. The surface shall be smooth and free of tool marks and ridges. Note: It is recommended that the prepared surface be coated with a drywall primer prior to the application of finish paint. See painting specification in this regard.

This level of finish is highly recommended where gloss, semigloss, enamel, or non-textured flat paints are specified or where severe lighting conditions occur. This highest quality finish is the most effective method of providing a uniform surface and minimizing the possibility of joint photographing and of fasteners showing through the final decoration.

Resources

TOOLS AND MATERIALS

AUTOMATIC TOOLS

Ames Tools • Supplies • Service
3305 Beckinridge Boulevard
Suite 122
Duluth, GA 30096
800-241-2771
www.amestools.com

Apla-Tech, Inc.
W2024 Industrial Drive #3
Kaukauna, WI 54130
800-827-3721
www.apla-tech.com

Hard Drywall, Inc.
PO Box 1259
7654 Bell Road
Windsor, CA 95492
800-867-8273
www.harddrywall.com

Renegade Tool
PO Box 971
1801 S. 21st Street
Parsons, KS 67357
888-921-5044
www.renegadetool.com

Wilco Tool
1122 Siddonsburg Road
Mechanicsburgh, PA 17055
717-766-6084

CORNERBEADS AND TAPERS

BPB Celotex
5301 West Cypress Street
Suite 300
Tampa, FL 33607
800-235-6839
www.bpb-celotex.com

Clinch-On Cornerbead
520 West Grove Avenue
Orange, CA 92865
714-637-4642

Con Form International, Inc.
11644 Fair Grove Industrial
   Boulevard
Maryland Heights, MO 63043
314-692-8999
www.straitflex.com

Flannery, Inc.
300 Parkside Drive
San Fernando, CA 91340
800-765-7585
www.flannerytrim.com

No•Coat
42 Elwood Road
Londonderry, NH 03053
888-662-6281
www.no-coat.com

Trim-Tex, Inc.
3700 Pratt Avenue
Lincoln, IL 60712
800-874-2333
www.trim-tex.com

USG Corporation
125 South Franklin Street
Chicago, IL 60606-4678
800-874-4968
www.usg.com

DRYWALL COMPANIES

BPB Celotex
5301 West Cypress Street
Suite 300
Tampa, FL 33607
800-235-6839
www.bpb-celotex.com

Georgia-Pacific Corporation
133 Peachtree Street, N.E.
Atlanta, GA 30303
800-225-6119
www.gp.com

James Hardie Gypsum
26300 La Alameda, Suite 250
Mission Viejo, CA 92691
800-426-3669
www.hardirock.com

LaFarge North America Inc.
12950 Worldgate Drive, Suite 400
Herndon, VA 20170-6001
703-480-3600
www.lafargenorthamerica.com

National Gypsum Company
2001 Rexford Road
Charlotte, NC 28211
800-628-4662
www.nationalgypsum.com

Raised Panel Designer Drywall
Pittcon Industries, Inc.
6409 Rhode Island Avenue
Riverdale, MD 20737-1098
800-637-7638
www.pittconnindustries.com

USG Corporation
125 South Franklin Street
Chicago, IL 60606
800-874-4968
www.usg.com

DRYWALL ROUTERS

DeWALT
PO Box 158
626 Hanover Pike
Hampstead, MD 21074
800-732-4447
www.dewalt.com

Porter-Cable Professional Power Tools
PO Box 2468
4825 Highway 45 North
Jackson, TN 38302-2468
800-487-8665
www.porter-cable.com

Roto Zip Tool Corporation
1861 Ludden Drive
Cross Plains, WI 53528
800-521-1871
www.rotozip.com

HAND TOOLS

E-Z Trowel
4505 West Hacienda
Las Vegas, NV 89118
866-397-6657
www.eztrowel.com

Hyde Manufacturing Co.
54 Eastford Road
Southbridge, MA 01550
800-331-5569
www.hydetools.com

Johnson Abrasives Co., Inc.
49 Fitzgerald Drive
Jaffrey, NH 03452
800-628-8005
(603-628-8005 in New Hampshire)
www.johnsonabrasives.com

Kraft Tool Co.
8325 Hedge Lane Terrace
Shawnee, KS 66227
800-422-2448
www.krafttool.com

Marshalltown Trowel Company
104 S. 8th Avenue
Marshalltown, IA 50158
515-753-0127
www.marshalltown.com

Stanley® Golblatt® Tools
The Stanley Works
1000 Stanley Drive
New Britain, CT 06053
(860) 225-5111
www.stanleyworks.com

Warner Tool
Warner™ Manufacturing Company
13435 Industrial Park Boulevard
Minneapolis, MN 55441
877-927-6372
www.warnertool.com

MISCELLANEOUS TOOLS

Back blocking device

Flat Fast, Inc.
1122 Siddonsburg Road
Mechanicsburg, PA 17055
717-766-6084
www.butthanger.com

Bench step

Mack's Step™
4686 Eagle Circle, NW
North Canton, OH 44720
888-586-8650
www.macksstep.com

Curved wall track

Flex-Ability Concepts
PO Box 7145
Edmond, OK 73083
405-715-1799
www.flexc.com

Drywall clips

Prest-on Company
312 Lookout Point
Hot Springs, AR 71913
800-323-1813
www.prest-on.com

Drywall lifts

Telpro™, Inc.
7251 South 42nd Street
Grand Forks, ND 58201
800-448-0822
www.telproinc.com

Dust-free sander

Porter-Cable
Professional Power Tools
PO Box 2468
4825 Highway 45 North
Jackson, TN 38302-2468
800-487-8665
www.porter-cable.com

Dust mask

3M
3M Center, Building 275-6W-01
PO Box 33275
St. Paul, MN 55133-3275
800-265-1840
www.3M.com/occsafety/

Electric box protectors

Sand Hollow Hardware, LLC
12586 Bridger Street, Suite 100
Boise, ID 83713
208-375-1533
www.sandhollowhardware.com

Plastic moldings

Canamould™ Extrusions Inc.
101A Roytec Road
Woodbridge, ON L4l 8A9
Canada
905-264-4436
www.canamould.com

Stilts and Benches

Dura-Stilt Sales
Limited Partnership
PO Box 271313
8316 SW 8th Street
Oklahoma, City, OK 73128
800-225-2440
www.durastilts.com

Temporary Wall Supports

Curtain Wall Company
490 Wellington Avenue
Cranston, RI 02910
800-424-8251
www.curtain-wall.com

ZipWall®
2464 Massachusetts Avenue
Cambridge, MA 02140
617-499-9966
www.zipwall.com

Texture repair spray

Spraytex, Inc.
28430 W. Witherspoon Parkway
Valencia, CA 91355
800-234-5979
www.spraytex.com

SCAFFOLDING

bil-jax
125 Taylor Parkway
Archbold, OH 43502
419-445-9675
www.bil-jax.com

Falcon Ladder and Scaffold
Manufacturing Ltd.
222 Adams Road
Kelowna, BC V1X 7R2
Canada
800-522-3313
www.falconscaffold.com

SCREWGUNS

DeWALT
PO Box 158
626 Hanover Pike
Hampstead, MD 21074
800-732-4447
www.dewalt.com

Grabber® Construction
Products
205 Mason Circle
Concord, CA 94520
800-477-8876
www.grabberman.com

Makita
14930 Northam Street
La Mirada, CA 90638
1-800-462-5482
www.makita.com

SENCO Products, Inc.
8485 Broadwell Road
Cincinnati, OH 45244
800-543-4596
www.senco.com

DRYWALL ASSOCIATIONS AND FURTHER READING

ASSOCIATIONS

AWCI
Association of the Wall and
Ceiling Industries
803 West Broad Street, Suite 600
Falls Church, VA 22046
703-534-8300
www.awci.org

Gypsum Association
810 First Street NE, Suite 510
Washington, DC 20002
202-289-5440
www.gypsum.org

FURTHER READING

USG Handbook
USG Corporation
125 South Franklin Street
Chicago, IL 60606
800-874-4968
www.usg.com

Index

A

Abuse-resistant drywall, 10
Abutting surface, fitting drywall to, 132–133
Accelerant, 99, 151
Access, planning for, 18–19
Acoustical ceiling textures, 165–166
Adhesive technique, 61–63
    for beads, 75–76
    for cement board, 139
    for moisture-resistant drywall, 139
    multiple layers of drywall, attaching,
        134, 141
Air bubbles, pitting caused by, 104–105
Angle applicator, 103
Angled walls, measuring, 51
Archway beads, 36, 126–128
Archways, 117, 124–128
Automatic taper, 101–102

B

Back-blocking, 129–131
Backing materials, 49–51
Baker's scaffold, 30
Bathrooms, 132–133.
    See also Moisture-resistant drywall
Beads, 37–38, 74
    archway, 36, 126–128
    bullnose (*See* Bullnose beads)
    cracked, 106
    inside corner, 36–37
    L-bead, 37–38, 133, 141
    metal (*See* Metal beads)
    for off angles, 36–37, 119–120
    outside corner
        (*See* Outside corner beads)
    paper-faced, 37, 75–77, 120
    vinyl (*See* Vinyl beads)
Beams, fitting drywall to, 132–133
Bending regular drywall, 123–126. *See also*
    Flexible drywall
Beveled trowels, 40–41, 84, 87–88, 97–98
Bowed studs or joists, replacing or
    straightening, 49
Bowing drywall, 63, 135
Bubbled tape, 105–106
Bullnose beads, 34, 36–37, 75–76, 120,
    126–128
Butted seams
    avoiding, 13–14, 59, 65, 67, 71
    back-blocking, 129–131
    large openings, elimination of,
        152–153
    location of, 59, 65, 70, 129
    ridging, 59, 129–131
    taping, 85–87, 89

C

Carrying drywall, 58
Cart, drywall, 58
Ceiling joists
    bowed, replacing or straightening, 49
    fastener spacing, 60

    panels parallel/perpendicular to,
        13, 64–66, 71
Ceiling panels
    attaching parallel/perpendicular to
        joists, 13, 64–66, 71
    floating corners technique, 61–62, 154
    hanging process, 59
    high-strength, 11
    insulation, attaching over rigid, 51
    lifting tools, 28–32
    multiple layers, attaching, 135–137
    sanding, 111
    taping process, 88, 91
Ceilings
    acoustical ceiling textures, 165–166
    furring with 1× 3s, 65
    garage, 71
    hanging process, 63–66
    high (cathedral), 11, 17, 64–65, 72
    sloped, 72
    straightening wavy or irregular, 49, 65
    truss uplift, problem of, 154
Cement board, 11–12, 17
    cutting round openings in, 138
    installing, 137–139
Chalkline, 24, 72
Cleanup, general, 114
Concave seams, 104, 111
Construction joints, 140
Control joints, 140
Corner
    beads (*See* Beads)
    floating corners technique, 61–62, 154
    inside (*See* Inside corner)
    off-angle (*See* Off-angle corners)
    out-of-plumb, fitting square
        panel into, 25
    outside (*See* Outside corner)
    rounded corners taping technique,
        120–123
Corner crimper, 35, 74–75
Corner finisher, adjustable, 102–103
Corner roller, 75, 77, 92, 102
Cost of job, 16
Cracked seams, 105
Crowned seams, 90, 104, 111
Curved trowels. *See* Beveled trowels
Curved walls, 123–124
Cutting process, 51–59
    large openings, 53–54, 68–69, 71
    panels, 52–53
    small openings, 55–59, 68–71, 138
Cutting tools, 24–28, 52–54. *See also*
    Saws; Utility knife

D

Decorating drywall, 158–170
    embossed surfaces, 141
    layered effects using L-bead, 141
    painting, 158–162
    texturing (*See* Texturing)
    wall coverings, 170

Doors
    buildouts, wrapping, 133
    cutting openings for, 53–54, 68, 71
    eliminating opening for, 152–153
    sanding around, 114
Dry-bending regular drywall, 125–126
Drying-type joint compound, 43–44, 82, 91
Dry sanding sponge, 46, 113–115
Drywall
    defined, 4–5
    grain orientation in, 66
    levels of finishing, 100
    size of panels (length/thickness), 5–13
    types and uses, 5–12
        (*See also specific types*)
Drywall cart, 58
Drywall hammer, 32, 139
Drywall lift, 29–30
Drywall rasp, 27, 53
Drywall router. *See* Router, drywall
Drywall sandpaper. *See* Sandpaper
Drywall saws. *See* Saws
Drywall screw gun, 32–33, 59–61
Drywall sponge, 46–47, 114–115
Dust, protection from, 108–109

E

Electrical outlet boxes
    cutting holes for, 55–59, 68–71
    eliminating, 149–151
    repairing overcut box, 146
    sanding around, 113–114
Estimates
    house, 17–18, 20–21
    materials, 15–18
    room, 16–17
    rough, 18
Expansion joints, 38

F

Fastening process, 59–63
    cement board, 139
    fire-resistant drywall, 137
    multiple layers of drywall, 134–135
Fastening tools and materials (fasteners),
    32–34, 45, 59–61. *See also* Nails;
    Screws
    for beads, 75–76
    concealing with joint compound, 80,
        83, 91, 99
    repairs, 142–144
    spacing of, 60
Fiberglass-mesh tape, 42–43
    abutting surfaces, fitting drywall to,
        132
    curved walls, use on, 124
    hole repair, 145–150
    inside corners, use on, 91, 93, 94
    off-angle corners, use on, 120–121
    taping method, 84–85
54-inch-wide drywall, 11, 14
Filler coat, joint compound, 87–89

inside corners, 95–96
outside corners, 97–99
reapplying, 111–112
Finish coat, joint compound, 79, 89–91
inside corners, 96, 102
outside corners, 99
reapplying, 111–112
Finishing, levels of, 100
Finish sanding, 111–114
Fire-resistant drywall, 8–10, 17
fastening, 137
multiple layers, 134
taping, 97
Fire-taping, 97
Flat boxes, 103
Flat taping, 132–133
Flexible drywall, 10–11
arched walls, used for, 124–126
curved walls, used for, 123
Floating corners technique, 61–62, 154
Foil-backed drywall, 11
Framing. *See also* Ceiling joists; Studs
maximum spacing (inches on center)
for, 6–11, 163
metal framing, attaching drywall to, 68
uneven, use of resilient
channel on, 132
wood framing, installing drywall over,
49–50
Framing square, 23, 51, 55–56
Furnace room, 97
Furring strips
on ceilings, prior to drywall
installation, 65
hole repair, 145–147
water damaged drywall, temporary
support for, 155

G

Gable walls, hanging, 72–73
Gaps, filling, 80–81, 94
Garages
fire-taping, 97
hanging drywall in, 71
Grain orientation, drywall, 66
Gypsum-core tile backer, 12

H

Hammer, drywall, 32
Hand-applied textures, 169–170
Hand sander, 46
Hanging process, 48–77
backing materials, 49–51
ceilings, 59, 63–66
cutting, 51–59
environmental conditions
needed for, 50
fastening drywall, 59–63
gable walls, 72–74
general guidelines, 59, 71
measuring, 51
metal framing, attaching drywall to, 68
trim accessories, 75–77
(*See also* Beads)
walls, 67–73
Hanging tools and materials, 23–38
beads (*See* Beads)
cutting tools, 24–28, 52–54
(*See also* Saws; Utility knife)
fastening tools and materials, 32–34,
45, 59–61
lifting tools, 28–32
(*See also* Panel lifter; Stilts)
measuring and marking tools, 23–24,
51, 55–56, 137
Hawks, 40, 84
Heat ducts, openings for, 59
Holes in drywall, repairing, 144–148
Horizontal layout, 14, 67–70
House, estimating materials for, 17–18,
20–21

I

Inside corner
beads, 36–37 (*See also* Beads)
sanding, 113–114
taping of, 79–80, 83, 91–96, 99, 102
Insulation
rigid, attaching drywall over, 51
wet insulation, removing, 155

J

Joint compound
abutting surfaces, fitting drywall to,
132–133
approximate coverage of materials, 45
for beads, 75, 77, 118–119
choosing correct, 44
coats of, 78–80 (*See also* Filler coat,
joint compound; Finish coat, joint
compound; Tape-embedding coat,
joint compound)
gaps, filling, 80–81, 94
hand-applied textures, use for, 169
hole repair, 145–150
large openings, elimination of,
152–153
mixing process, 81–83, 105
mixing tools, 45–46, 81–82
multiple layers of drywall, attaching,
134–135
rounded corners, use for, 120–123
spray texturing, used for, 167–168
types of, 43–45 (*See also* Drying-type
joint compound; Setting-type joint
compound)
Joint-compound loading pumps, 103
Joints
construction, 140
control, 140
expansion, 38
unnecessary, elimination of, 13
Joint tape
approximate coverage of, 45
types of, 41–43 (*See also* Fiberglass-
mesh tape; Paper tape)
Joists. *See* Ceiling joists
J-trims, 37–38

K

Kitchens, use of moisture-resistant drywall
in. *See* Moisture-resistant drywall
Knockdown texture
roller texture (hand-applied), 169
spray application, 166, 168–169

L

Large holes, repairing, 145–148
Large openings
cutting, 53–54, 68–69, 71
eliminating, 152–153
Laundry room.
See Moisture-resistant drywall
Layered drywall, 134–137, 141
Layout guidelines, 13–14, 16
L-bead, 37–38, 133, 141
Lift, drywall, 29–30
Lifting tools, 28–32.
See also Panel lifter; Stilts

M

Marking tools, 23–24
Material list, 15–18
Materials, accessory.
See Tools and materials
Measuring of walls/ceilings, 16, 51
gable walls, 72
openings, holes for, 53, 55–57
tools, 23–24, 51, 55–56, 137
Mechanical taping, 101–103
Mesh tape. *See* Fiberglass-mesh tape
Metal beads, 38, 74–77, 96–97
cracked, 106
off-angle corners, 120
Metal framing, attaching drywall to, 68

Mildew damage, 156
Moisture-resistant drywall, 7–8, 17, 139
Mud boxes, 103
Multilayer applications, 134–137, 141

N

Nails, 32–34, 60–61
approximate number needed, 45
concealing heads of, 80, 83, 91, 99
depressions, repair of, 143–144
galvanized nails for cement board, 139
multiple layers of drywall, attaching,
135
popped, 106, 142–143
repairing nail holes, 144–145
sanding heads of, 110–111

O

Off-angle corners
beads for, 36–37, 118–120
rounded corners technique, 120–123
taping, 118–123
Openings, cutting holes for, 53–59
in cement board, 138–139
large openings, 53–54, 68–69, 71
round openings, 56–57, 138
small openings, 55–59, 68–71, 138
Openings, eliminating, 149–153
Orange peel texture, 166–168
Out-of-plumb corner, fitting panel to, 24–25
Outside corner
hanging panels on, 70–71
taping process, 83, 96–99
Outside corner beads, 34–36, 74. *See also*
Beads; Off-angle corners, beads for
cracked, 106
taping, 83, 96–97

P

Painting, 158–162
drywall yellowing, problem of, 160
hand-applied textures, 169–170
photographing, problem of, 104, 159
prime coat, 159, 163
techniques, 160–162
textured ceilings, 166
top coat, 104, 160
Paint roller
finish coat of joint compound, application of, 90–91, 122
hand-applied textures, application of,
169
paint application, 160–161
water, application of, 124
Paneling, attaching drywall over, 51
Panel lifter, 28–29, 64–65, 68, 70
Paper-faced beads, 37, 75–77, 120
Paper tape, 41–42
bubbled or loose, 105–106
curved walls, use on, 124
hole repair, 146, 149
inside corners, use on, 91–92
large openings, elimination of,
152–153
use of, 85–87
Photographing, 104, 159
Pitting, 104–105
Planning drywall job, 13–21
access for materials, planning for,
18–19
estimating materials, 15–18, 20–21
layout guidelines, 13–14, 16
Plaster, attaching drywall over, 51
Pocket Kart, 58
Pole sander, 46, 109–111, 122
Popcorn ceilings, 165
Pre-bowing drywall, 63, 135
Prybar, 28, 68

R

Rasp, drywall, 27, 53
Ready-mixed joint compound, 82–83,
120–121

Recommended Levels of Gypsum Board Finish, 100, 171–173
Remodeling repairs, 149–153
Repairs, 142–156
    fastener depressions, 143–144
    holes in drywall, 144–148
    mildew, 156
    popped nails and screws, 142–143
    remodeling, 149–153
    stress cracks, 154–155
    textured surfaces, 166
    water damage, 155–156
Resilient channel, 132, 136
Ridging
    butted seams, 129–131
    construction joints, 140
Roller textures, 169
Roof trusses, uplift of, 154
Room, estimating materials for, 16–17
Rough coat, joint compound. *See* Tape-embedding coat, joint compound
Rough estimate, house, 18
Round openings, cutting holes for, 56–57, 138
Router, drywall, 28, 53, 56, 69

S

Sanders and sanding materials, 46–47.
    See also Sanding screens; Sandpaper
    dust-free sanders, 116
    pole sanders, 46, 109–111, 122
    sponges, 46–47, 113–115
Sanding process, 78, 107–116, 122
    cleanup, 114
    crowned seams, 104
    finish sanding, 111–114
    oversanding, 112
    pole sanding, 46, 109–111, 122
    preparation for, 108–109
    prior to third coat, 89–90
    wet sanding, 47, 115
Sanding screens, 47, 90, 109, 113, 122
Sandpaper, 47, 89–90, 109–110, 113, 122
Saws, 69
    drywall, 27–28, 53
    drywall utility, 27, 53, 55–57
Scaffolds, 30–31
Screw gun, drywall, 32–33, 59–61
Screws, 32–34, 59–61
    approximate number needed, 45
    cement board, use with, 139
    concealing heads of, 80, 83, 91, 99
    depressions, repair of, 143–144
    layering drywall, 141
    multiple layers of drywall, attaching, 135
    popped, 106, 142–143
    sanding heads of, 110–111
Scriber, 24
Seams, butted. *See* Butted seams
Seams, taping, 84–91, 99, 105
    butted-end seams, 87–89
    first coat, 84–87
    mesh-tape method, 84–85
    paint-roller application, 91
    paper-tape method, 85–87
    second coat, 87–89
    tapered-edge seams, 87–89
    taping-knife application, 90–91
    third coat, 89–91
Setting-type joint compound, 44–45, 81–82, 84, 87
    hand-applied textures, use for, 169
    large openings, elimination of, 152
    moisture-resistant drywall, use with, 139
    off-angle corners, use for, 120–121
    one-day taping method, 99
    small openings, elimination of, 151
Shrinking seams, 105
Size of panels (length/thickness), 5–12

Skim coat, 79, 99–101, 104, 159
Small holes, repairing, 144–145
Small openings
    cutting holes for, 55–59, 68–71, 138
    eliminating, 149–151
Solid backing, 51
Sound attenuation
    acoustical ceiling textures, 165–166
    multiple drywall layers for, 134
    resilient channel for, 136
Sponges, sanding, 46–47, 113–115
Sprayed textures. *See* Texturing
Spray painting, 161–162
Stairways, construction joint in, 140
Step-up benches, 29–30, 63–64
"Stiff arm" tool. *See* T-support
Stilts, 31–32, 64, 80, 88, 111
Stress cracks, 154–155
Studs
    bowed, replacing or straightening, 49
    fastener spacing, 60
    hanging panels parallel/perpendicular to, 13, 135
    maximum spacing (inches on center), 6–11, 163
    spacing for curved walls, 123
Switches
    cutting holes for, 55–59
    repairing overcut hole, 146

T

Tape-embedding coat, joint compound, 79, 84–87
    inside corners, 92–95
    outside corners, 97
Tape measure, 23
Tapered-edge seams, 87–89
Tape reel (holder), 42–43
Taping knife, 39, 41, 75, 77, 84, 86–87
    abutting surfaces, fitting drywall to, 132–133
    butted-end seams, taping, 89
    double-edged, 93
    electric boxes, cleaning out, 114
    finish coat, application of, 90–91
    hole repair, 150
    inside corners, taping, 92–93, 95–96
    outside corners, taping, 97–99
    rounded corners, use for, 121–123
Taping process, 78–106. *See also* Seams, taping
    basics, 78–81
    at ceiling level, 88
    crowned seams, checking for, 90
    curved walls, 124
    environmental conditions for, 80
    fastener heads, concealing, 80, 83, 91, 99
    hand taping compared to mechanical taping, 101
    inside corners, 79–80, 83, 91–96, 99, 102
    mechanical taping, 78, 101–103
    mixing joint compound, 81–83
    off-angle corners, 118–123
    one-day taping, 99
    outside corners, 83, 96–99
    preparation for, 80–81
    problems of, 90, 104–106, 111
    rounded corners technique, 120–123
    seams, 84–91, 99, 105
    sequence for, 83, 99
    skim coating, 99–101
    what to tape, 79–80
Taping tools and materials, 38–46
    approximate coverage of materials, 45
    joint compound (*See* Joint compound)
    joint tape, 41–43, 45 (*See also* Fiberglass-mesh tape; Paper tape)
    mechanical taping tools, 41

mixing tools, 45–46, 81
    tape reel (holder), 42–43
    trowels (*See* Trowels)
Texturing, 162–170
    acoustical ceiling textures, 165–166
    application, 163–165
    environmental conditions for, 165
    general guidelines, 162
    hand-applied, 169–170
    knockdown texture, 166, 168–169
    orange-peel texture, 166–168
    overspray, protection from, 164
    preparation, 163
    repairs to, 166
    sprayed-on wall textures, 166–169
Tile, backing for, 12.
    See also Moisture-resistant drywall
Tools and materials, 22–47.
    See also specific tools and materials
    cutting tools, 24–28, 52–54
    expansion joints, 38
    fastening tools (*See* Fastening tools and materials [fasteners])
    lifting tools, 28–32
    measuring and marking tools, 23–24
    sanding tools and materials (*See* Sanders and sanding materials)
    taping tools, 38–46, 81
Trestles. *See* Step-up benches
Triangular sander, 46, 113–114
Trim beads, 37–38. *See also* L-bead
Trim snips, 74
Troll, The, 58
Trowels, 84, 90, 92, 121–122, 135
    care of, 40
    hand-trowel texturing, 169
    types of, 38–41 (*See also* Beveled trowels; Taping knife)
Truss uplift, 154
T-square, 23–24, 72, 137
T-support, 28–29, 64, 155
Tub/shower unit, fitting drywall to, 132–133

U

Urethane insulation, attaching drywall over rigid, 51
Utility knife, 26–27, 52–54
    cement board, cutting, 137–139
    V-groove, forming, 154
Utility room, 97. *See also* Moisture-resistant drywall
Utility saw. *See* Saws

V

Vacuum cleaner, wet/dry, 114
Vapor retarders, 8, 139
Vents, openings for, 59
Vertical layout, 14, 67
Vinyl beads, 75–77, 118–120, 126–128, 141

W

Wall coverings, 170
Walls
    hanging, 67–73
    width/height of, panel hanging based on, 13–14, 67
Water damage, 155–156
Water stains, 156
Wet-bending regular drywall, 123–125
Wet sanding, 47, 115
Windows
    buildouts, wrapping, 133
    cutting openings for, 53–54, 68–69
    eliminating opening for, 152–153
    L-bead used for window jamb, 133
    sanding around, 114
Wood framing, 49–50

Y

Yellowing of drywall, 160